TQM In Action

One Firm's Journey Toward Quality and Excellence

TQM In Action

One Firm's Journey Toward Quality and Excellence

Joseph V. Walker
Barbara L. Ciaramitaro
Plunkett & Cooney, PC.
Detroit, Michigan

American Bar Association
Section of Law Practice Management

The Section of Law Practice Management, American Bar Association, offers an educational program for lawyers in practice. Books and other materials are published in furtherance
of that program. Authors and editors of publications may express their own legal inter-
pretations and opinions, which are not necessarily those of either the American Bar
Association or the Section of Law Practice Management unless adopted pursuant to the
By-laws of the Association. The opinions expressed do not reflect in any way a position of
the Section or the American Bar Association.

Library of Congress Catalog Card Number 93-073323
ISBN 0-89707-923-X

94 95 96 97 98   5 4 3 2 1

Discounts are available for books ordered in bulk. Special consideration is given to
state bars, CLE programs, and other bar-related organizations. Inquire at Publications
Planning and Marketing, American Bar Association, 750 N. Lake Shore Drive, Chicago,
Illinois 60611.

Table of Contents

The 1990s ushered in a wave of introspection among lawyers as to the relationship among themselves, their services, and their clients. Changes in the economics of law practice, attitudes about lawyers, and society at large abruptly forced many law firms out of decades of complacency about the nature and quality of their work.

Among the concepts that were discussed with increasing regularity during this period were "quality," "client-centered lawyering," "satisfaction," and "standards of service." The realization that law firms need to focus on quality in order to prosper prompted many forward thinking practitioners to look outside the profession for guidance. What they discovered was a burgeoning movement in the business community called "Total Quality Management" (TQM). The theories upon which TQM was based were pioneered by W. Edwards Deming, J.M. Juran, and others from as far back as the 1930s; embraced by Japanese industrialists after World War II; and popularized in the United States in the 1980s.

Although TQM principles were applied in a variety of industries, observers questioned whether they could be transferred to a professional services industry like law. The first book that assured they could was *The Quality Pursuit,* edited by Robert Michael Greene and published by the ABA Section of Law Practice Management in 1989. That laid the groundwork for much of the commentary that followed.

The emerging consensus seemed to be that a focus on continual improvement in the quality of legal services as defined by client satisfaction was critical to the success of law firms and other legal services organizations. There was to be sure much talk but less action.

Enter Joe Walker and Barbara Ciaramitaro of Plunkett & Cooney in Detroit. Walker's firm decided to try TQM for themselves. They did NOT hire a consulting firm to tell them what to do. They did it the old-fashioned way: They learned it. Even more importantly, they kept notes and wrote about their experiences, and out of that came—in clear, concise prose—a step-by-step, tried-and-true plan for implementing TQM in a firm.

TQM in Action should be required reading for all law firms and their managers. Both small and large firms will learn the fundamental keys of practice improvement through TQM. With this book practitioners have the tools to make decisions about how they provide services and to implement a program that will assure not just quality, but economic viability in a competitive world.

Professor Gary A. Munneke
Chair, LPM Publishing

Preface

We love the Motown sound. Over the years, we have heard the Temptations' hit "Ball of Confusion" played and replayed. Although it was written in 1970, you can listen to it today and still find parts of it current—"Politicians say more taxes will solve everything"!

The day-to-day providing of legal services by a law firm during the 1980s sometimes seemed like a "ball of confusion." Legal literature told us that the work of highly accomplished professional and ethical attorneys, more frequently than was acceptable, did not meet the clients' perception of what was effective and efficient. No one knew where the legal services world was headed as we neared the end of the decade. But it didn't seem to matter to law firms because the early and mid-1980s saw unprecedented growth in the profession. Wouldn't it just continue?

There was no need to fix anything because nothing appeared to be broken. Revenues climbed. The law schools continued to fill, and the great numbers finishing law school were absorbed easily into the profession.

However, with the recession starting late in the decade, we realized that the growth would not be unlimited and that the inefficiencies and overall high cost of legal services, which were coming under great scrutiny, needed to be addressed in a new way.

Management ideas were creeping into the profession. Clients were challenging us to lower our costs and to manage the providing of legal services in a better way. Manage? That concept was virtually unknown in the profession, at least not in any traditional business-school sense. While corporations struggled to *change* management models to meet the threat of the recession, the legal profession struggled to *accept* management models. It was becoming apparent, however, that corporate or institutional clients were going to insist on management of their matters. In addition, they were going to insist that law firms manage their own affairs better, so that the ever-increasing costs experienced by law firms of all sizes would not automatically be passed on to clients in the form of higher fees and expenses.

What are you doing about starting salaries for associates? What training are you providing them? Are you using technology to the fullest? Are you delegating my matters to the appropriate level—associate, paralegal? Are your teams working efficiently? These and other questions were being asked directly of law firm managers.

With all these challenges staring them in the face, law firm managers found themselves ill-equipped to solve these problems either quickly or easily.

Managers of law firms, small or large, generally had no formal management training. They got into positions of authority in their firms by becoming partners or shareholders (as a result of being outstanding lawyers, not managers); and later in their careers they moved into the highest levels of management, usually because of their seniority. This did

Evolution, revolution, gun control, the sound of soul, shootin' rockets to the moon, kids growing up too soon.

Politicians say more taxes will solve everything . . .

Round and around and around we go where the world's headed nobody knows.

"Ball of Confusion"

("That's What the World Is Today")

—The Temptations

not necessarily make for good management. Additionally, traditional law firm hierarchies and cultures were understandably resistant to transforming their profession into a business.

As an organization, we recognized that a cultural change could be accomplished that met client needs. The road that every law firm longed to travel (the highway to quality and efficiency in legal services) was winding, potholed, and at times unpaved! We recognized that we needed to change, but our firm culture was comfortable with "business as usual." Some things needed to change; but some people wanted them to stay the same.

The journey we took, and we hope you will begin, is recounted in this story about one law firm's endeavor to straighten and pave the road. It's about revolution, evolution. . . .

We readily admit that not everything contained here is revolutionary. Many of the ideas and programs are, in fact, well known. What is revolutionary is that together they can constitute a total quality program—or, more appropriately, a process—that can be put into action quickly and in a comprehensive way. The plan we proposed was total quality for us and for our clients. The elements of your plan may be vastly different. Our plan was also "homegrown"; not everyone's should be, however. There are many qualified consultants you can consider for help.

Whatever approach you choose, what you will find here is one roadmap for cultural change and a total quality process that is designed for information feedback into your organization to help you attain continuous quality improvement. That is where you will experience gain and your clients will experience ever-increasing levels of satisfaction.

A few words about our goal for this book. Throughout its history, Plunkett & Cooney has always "given back," whether through Bar Association activities, pro bono work, or civic or charitable endeavors. It's time to do it again. Our goal, therefore, is to share our story, our journey, and our process (which we call Excellence in Action^SM)* so that quality and efficient legal services can be made available to all who seek them, whether the seekers are from small, medium, or large law firms or from corporate legal staffs. District attorney, public defender, city attorney, and pro bono legal staffs can benefit, too.

What you must have is the commitment to read, listen, and react to what you hear, to develop a plan and have the courage to see it through.

Perhaps you have taken the first step by reading this book. We know that lawyers skim through anything that isn't meant for a client. Therefore, we have intentionally kept our message brief. At the end of each chapter, you will find tips for "Making It All Happen." Show that part of this book to leaders in your firm, leaders who are open-minded and flexible thinkers and who can participate with you to be "change agents." It will lead them down the total quality path. For the ultimate in brevity, see Appendix A. For fun along the way, you will see some familiar lyrics from Motown hits. Enjoy your journey.

---

*Excellence in Action^SM is claimed as a service mark by Plunkett & Cooney, P.C.

Acknowledgments

Although it is not possible to acknowledge every person who helped make Excellence in Action and this book happen, our heartfelt thanks go out to each and every one of them. There are a few people and organizations, however, who deserve special recognition.

At Plunkett & Cooney we wish to acknowledge Paul Brakora—he was a "change agent" for the firm long before we knew we needed one; B. I. Stanczyk and David P. Ruwart—for their valuable critique and support; Kris Davis—who worked the manuscript and provided ongoing editing; and Colleen Goslin—whose commitment and enthusiasm epitomizes what Excellence in Action is all about.

Our thanks also to Alvin Greene, President and Chief Executive Officer of the American Law Firm Association (ALFA), for his review and critique.

It was our good fortune to work with Carol Siedell of the ABA who was our editor. Her suggestions were excellent.

We also acknowledge Bassett & Bassett, our communications consultants; Market Strategies, Inc., who assisted us with our Client Survey; and Human Resource Advisors, for the assistance with our Employee Survey.

There are two other people who use the words Excellence in Action to describe what they do. Rich Willis has his Excellence in Action Inc., a real estate promotional company in Columbia, Maryland, and Peter Orgain of Strafford, Vermont, uses the term to describe his self-improvement programs. Our thanks to both Rich and Peter for allowing us the use of the words to describe our TQM program for legal services providers.

Finally, our thanks to CPP/Belwin, Inc., for granting permission to use the lyrics from various Motown hits.

Dedication

We dedicate this book to the following people:

To my dad, Salvatore A. Ciaramitaro, Jr., who has taught me, by example, that excellence is not achieved through isolated acts or deeds, but only through the way you choose to live your life.
Barbara

To my friend and partner, Jon Kopit. Jon had MS and was our firm's private hero. He was and will remain our constant source of inspiration.
Joe

To the women and men of Plunkett & Cooney. They are this book. Thanks for "Making It All Happen."
Joe and Barbara

Revolution

The Danger of "Business as Usual"

Plunkett & Cooney was typical of many successful law firms in the 1980s. We were listed among the top 250 firms in the nation and the top five in Michigan. We had diversified, increased our number and type of clients, branched out, and provided the kind of client service that retained major long-term clients and provided an acceptable standard of living for our employees. We had a well-entrenched bonus system that rewarded performance at year's end, much to everyone's satisfaction.

At Plunkett & Cooney, we kept our ears to the ground, listening to developments in the profession—and near the end of the 1980s, the legal marketplace was indeed changing. As the 1990s began, a survey of legal and business periodicals confirmed the prediction. That awareness and the firm's constant communication with clients led us to believe there were some tough years ahead.

During the 1980s the firm introduced some basic management concepts—a yearly budget, for one. Our annual budgetary process was involved, sometimes intricate, based on facts, empirical data, and best guesses. As the last half of the decade played out, we were always within a percentage point of our predicted profitability. Our confidence in our budget process was very high, and we found that this was where the first evidence of change became obvious. Specifically, our 1991 budget predicted a major drop in our bottom-line profits.

Early warning went out to the partners (shareholders), but after so many prosperous years most did not believe that it could be so. Why the drop? What was going on? As the year unfolded and the dire prediction became a reality, many questions arose. And as the year's end approached, what normally was a happy time of year became unhappy. Bonuses were substantially lower. We had a crisis on our hands. Employees became fearful and discouraged. Fingers were pointed: it must be the fault of management; lack of leadership; overstaffing; lazy workers; too much expansion; too little expansion. The accusations went on and on. No one wanted to believe that the real cause was out of our hands. The world itself was

How do I say good-bye to what we had?

The good times that made us laugh, outweighed the bad —

I thought we'd get to see forever but forever has blown away

It's so hard to say good-bye to yesterday.

**"It's So Hard to Say Goodbye to Yesterday"
—Boys II Men**

changing, especially economically, and the legal world was not exempt from its effects. Something had to be done—for both the short and the long terms. Our comfortable existence was threatened in a real way. We needed to change. Business as usual signaled danger.

What was happening? Major clients were consolidating the number of firms they would use. Their goal: more control over their service providers. The economy was not just in the doldrums, it was in a full-fledged recession. Although your authors are not experts on this subject, others have written that this was the first time since the Great Depression that the economy had perceptibly affected law firms and their profitability in a negative way. In our firm's experience, earlier downturns in the economy still had produced an abundance of paying legal work. Not so this time around.

Long-time clients of the firm froze fees; others asked for and received across-the-board reductions, sometimes stated as percentages. On the expense side, large investments in people, technology, and resources still tugged on the firm's finances.

By some measures Plunkett & Cooney was fortunate. Several medium-size (by Michigan standards) law firms were forced to close their doors. Other law firms were "downsizing." Plunkett & Cooney was not immune to these difficult times either. It suffered some defections and internal upheaval, but overall, it maintained a steady hand on its head count and profitability.

Competition for new business was at an all-time high. There was (and still is) a glut of attorneys in the marketplace. Although Plunkett & Cooney responded to requests for proposals, or RFPs, to provide legal services for prospective clients, our responses in categories other than fees seemed overlooked. Business often went to those who simply quoted the lowest fees or had the best political connections. Client sophistication was at an all-time high. Clients knew what they wanted and knew what they wanted to pay for it. In short, clients were saying "I can hire any lawyer I want. Therefore, I want the best, at the lowest cost." How could we guarantee that we would be the firm of first choice for clients in terms of quality legal services at a fair price?

We began to assess what needed to be done inside our firm to achieve that goal. The obstacles were clear. We knew the legal profession was a culture that was resistant to change and, furthermore, many in our firm lacked a thorough understanding of the need for change.

We were also inexperienced with teamwork concepts. It wasn't that people didn't work together, it was just that they were not used to working in teams. There was a resistance to technology and a lack of understanding of what it could do. Leadership, mentorship, and training skills were underdeveloped, and generally our people did not see a connection between their behavior and the recognition and rewards they received. It was time for a change—revolutionary change.

We knew we had to redefine client service and improve our quality, but where should we start? What do you look for—specifically? We started in our own backyard.

Surveys and Focus Groups

With "redefining client service" as our goal, we needed hard and fast information, not unrelated anecdotes. We started, therefore, with an employee survey (see Appendix B), followed by focus groups (small discussion groups that solicited suggestions and opinions) at the professional support staff level.

Why did we start with our professional support staff? They, perhaps more than anyone, were closest to the action—the day-to-day provision of service. They knew the sources of client frustration and could help us understand it quickly and easily. They knew the barriers and obstacles to providing prompt efficient service. We suspected that our employees knew where problem areas were, both inside and outside the firm.

Our Professional Support Staff Survey asked: Did they have all the "tools" they needed? Did they know the "steps" to take to be efficient? Did they have the proper training to be productive, which to us means producing a consistent quality work product that exceeds the client's expectation—all at a reasonable cost? How did they view their jobs? Was their effort recognized?

We learned many things *from* our employees through this survey, and its results became the springboard for many of our later programs and changes.

We also learned some things *about* our employees through this survey. We learned, for example, that there were some significant differences in the attitudes of employees, depending on how many years they had worked with the firm. Our employees of longest standing felt a greater loyalty to the firm, which was reflected in a greater sense of ownership and allegiance to the firm's goals. This was demonstrated in how they viewed and did their jobs. But we found that the category of three- to five-year employees had less positive attitudes toward their work and the firm. They did not feel as strongly committed to the firm's goals. We looked for reasons for these differences. Maybe, we thought, it was because they had joined the firm during its most rapid period of growth and expansion and had never experienced the small-firm "family" feeling that had been so much a part of our culture. Whatever the cause, we knew we now had to create an organization in which everyone could feel a strong sense of commitment, loyalty, and a common sense of purpose.

After we compiled and reviewed the results of the employee survey, we formed focus groups of somewhat randomly selected groups of employees. These groups came from all levels of the firm, and we ensured that each group was representative of our employees. Individual groups were not stacked with people of like minds, attitudes, or skill levels.

Through these groups, we discussed the results of the survey and many of our ideas for change. Through the give and take of discussion, the beginnings of our total quality program began to take root.

We also did an In-House Attorney Survey (see Appendix C). From this process we were able to assess how our lawyers viewed our different practice areas. In this survey we also asked them to offer opinions from a marketing standpoint on what would be effective in retaining, if not expanding, our market share. We asked them to describe what problem areas they saw that represented barriers and obstacles to effective client service. We learned from their perspective what areas of the firm needed improvement.

An overall benefit of the lawyer survey was its universality. After all, it was a survey of our lawyers about our clients and our problems. Who could argue with that! To ensure universality, we asked for and received 100 percent compliance in the survey.

In many ways the answers we heard from our lawyers about our practice areas echoed and supported "management's" view. As a result, we could use the results of the lawyer survey to "sell" ideas for realigning personnel, for pricing our services, for techniques for marketing to new and existing clients, and for correcting problem service areas.

The statement has been made that "Success ties you to the past."[1] Both surveys convinced us that we needed to listen and react in different ways both to our employees and to our clients. They confirmed our belief that we needed to redefine client service; more to the point, we needed to recognize that clients were redefining it for us. It was not going to be business as usual.

We now had the inside view of the problem areas, and it was a good start, but we recognized that we were hearing from the backseat drivers. It was time to let the frontseat drivers—our clients—have the day and turn the car in the direction that they wanted it to go. We already knew a few things. We knew we needed to refine our understanding of client needs and to understand that clients today value the process involved in providing legal services as highly as they value the outcome. As for cost, for many of them it was too high. For clients, watching from the sidelines was a thing of the past. In short, client service was more than a favorable verdict or a technically correct contract. Clients wanted a say in calling the plays.

Client Satisfaction Surveys

To get the full picture, we really needed to know what the clients thought. We had read about Client Satisfaction Surveys, but how do you conduct one? Our clients seemed to have become more sophisticated in their use of RFPs, so why not develop one of our own to help in selecting a firm to conduct a Client Satisfaction Survey?

With some thought and research, we developed an RFP (see Appendix D). We intentionally kept it open and unstructured to allow for a wide range of responses. We chose four firms, and got four quality responses that had enough similarity to assure us we were on the right track; but each also had its own distinguishing characteristics that taught us something new.

The four interviews that followed introduced us to a new world of information: statistics and analysis. We intentionally selected a group that had no law firm experience, because we wanted a fresh, not canned, approach that was specific to our clients and our firm.

We embarked on a studied course consisting of executive interviews of ten representative clients from different practice areas; a telephone survey of 300 randomly selected additional clients; and finally, a mail survey to the rest of the client list.

Needless to say, we learned a lot from the client survey. Areas for improvement were easy to find among the data. We learned our technical proficiency was very high (we got high marks on "competent in specialty" and "unquestionable competence"). Where we fell down was on the soft items—the service items like "delivered when promised" and "timely delivery." Other results were more problematical and sometimes contradictory. "Your bills have too much detail." "There is not enough detail in your billing."

The results also revealed some communications problems with our clients. For example, they detailed a lack of promptness in returning telephone calls and complained that they sometimes got lost in our voice-mail system. They also told us that the clarity and timeliness of our billing process was not always the best. These and other areas for improvement became apparent. On the upside we found that generally speaking, our fee schedule was acceptable, and we even identified a few clients who were willing to accept a fee increase.

All in all, we were pleased with the outcome of the survey but also recognized its limitations. We recognized that a survey of our own clients would have a tendency to be positive; otherwise, these clients wouldn't be using our services in the first place. But even with this positive bias, we now had hard information to improve our services and to develop our process for total quality.

The business publications of the day chronicled the total quality management movement—some efforts were successful, some failed. A total quality effort for a law firm, of course, would, first of, all be unheard of and second, would be resisted, because lawyering constitutes a profession, not a business. What was needed, therefore, was a well-thought-out plan for cultural change. Although it's hard to say goodbye to yesterday, we could now do so because we had information about what tomorrow should look like.

Making It All Happen

1. Educate your firm about the changing legal marketplace. Circulate articles. Some say they are self-fulfilling prophecies, but everyone is reading them, including your clients.

2. Talk to everyone in your firm. Get out of your office, walk around. Listen.

3. Do an in-house survey of your support personnel such as the one in Appendix B. It is a beginning step to establishing total quality in your organization. But don't just gather the information, act on it.

4. Set up focus groups at all levels (partners, associates, paralegals, professional support staff, administrative staff) to find the areas of the firm that need improvement; get the nuts and bolts ideas for client service improvement. You may want an outside consultant to conduct these sessions so that frank discussion will flow.

5. Do an in-house lawyer survey such as the one in Appendix C. It will help you see the big picture from the inside. It can easily be adapted and improved to fit your organization.

6. Gather information through periodic client meetings. Do you sit down at least once a quarter with your top fifty clients and discuss their business with them? What are their plans for the future? How are they currently defining quality legal service? By your responsiveness? Your technical abilities? Your bill or fees? Find out.

7. Review all current client guidelines provided to you by clients for the handling of their matters. Do you see a trend?

8. Gather all current RFPs or statements of qualifications and comb them for constant themes.

9. Develop an RFP of your own to engage a market survey firm. (See Appendix D for an example). If you have the resources to do it in-house, you may want to do so. However, there is a good argument that clients will be more forthcoming with information if it is being gathered by an independent third party who will respect the clients' choice of anonymity.

10. Develop the habit of long-term thinking (vision).

11. Document all of the above and write or rewrite the firm's mission statement or guiding principles as a result of what you have learned.

Every organization needs a goal, a mission. The mission statement acts as a set of principles that will guide the organization on its journey. It must be written, and it must be constantly visible. Consequently, the goal and mission will remain in focus and the future direction will always have a guide. One caveat: Don't write it in stone. Things are changing too fast.

Chapter 2

Developing the Action Plan

John Marshall, Benjamin Cardozo, Thurgood Marshall, are all legendary heros of the legal profession. But do you recognize these heros: W. Edwards Deming, Joseph M. Juran, Philip B. Crosby? They are recognized quality gurus. Take some time to read about them. Your clients know who they are. You should too. More important, you should know why and where their thinking started, and what they are saying today. *The Total Quality Handbook*[1] is a good start.

Stories in the book recount how individuals in companies utilized the gurus' "points," "steps," "absolutes," or "tools" to create total quality programs. The point to be made here is there is lots of help out there in books and articles, and there are plenty of quality consultants who have a lot to offer. At first, the relevance of most that is written may not be apparent, but a little study will be very worthwhile.

TQM (Total Quality Management), Self-Directed Work Teams, Zero Defects, Mission Statements, Vision, Empowerment, Paradigm Shift —all are management buzzwords of the 1990s. Total Quality, however, is *not* just a buzzword, *not* just a program: It is really a process. It goes to the very heart of how you do business. For starters, the best thing you can do is eliminate the words *total quality* from your vocabulary until you define what quality means to your clients and your organization. Then, and only then, can you go back to these words and figure out what they really mean and whether they can be useful in developing your action plan for achieving your goals.

For a variety of reasons, the legal services world is only now adopting some of the concepts that have long been a part of the TQM movement in the business world. (Recently, Vice-President Gore completed his report on Reinventing Government. If TQM has reached into the ranks of government, even the most skeptical must pay heed.) Even so, the profession is at least three to five years behind the times. This can cause problems in determining where and how to begin. For example, there is a strong popular movement toward "empowering" individual employees to "break the rules" when necessary to provide high-quality service. We found in our organization that to begin with such "empowerment" would cause havoc. We had not even determined what the "rules" were so we

As I walk this land with broken dreams

I have visions of many things...

I know I've got to find some kind of peace of mind,

I'll be searching ev'ry-where

just to find someone to care.

I'll be looking ev'ryday;

I know I'm gonna find a way.

Nothing's gonna stop me now;

I'll find a way some-how...

"What Becomes of the Broken Hearted"
—Jimmy Ruffin

could allow our employees to "break" them when necessary. Our goal, of course, is true employee empowerment, but first we had to build a strong framework of quality standards and expectations.

The message here is to be very cautious against just dropping in the most popular TQM technique without a foundation. Spend the time to know and understand your organization, its problems, and its people. Spend the time to thoroughly understand the reasons behind popular TQM techniques and programs. Determine where you want your organization to be in two, five, and ten years, and then strategize on how to get there step by step. This is what developing an action plan is all about.

Despite mounting (overwhelming?) evidence toward the end of the 1980s that the legal marketplace was changing, it was still a challenge to achieve consensus that the danger of doing business as usual was a real threat to our firm. Moving a large (or for that matter, any size) institution to action is like teaching an elephant to dance. But all will agree that even the first steps toward change will require a well-thought-out plan of attack. We also knew that the changes we envisioned as necessary for our firm's survival would have an impact on every person and challenge every aspect of our thoughts of "business as usual." So here was our plan and approach.

Mobilizing Your "Change Agents"

Our first step was to develop a core group of people (known in today's jargon as *change agents*) who would be involved in strategizing and implementing our plan, which we called "Excellence in Action" (EIA). Although this happened without much planning, we now are convinced that the success or failure of your plan for change is directly related to the commitment and energy of your "change agents." They must understand thoroughly the long-term goals of your plan, adopt them as their own, and be, at times, oblivious to the inevitable resistance.

At our firm, the core EIA group consisted of the president/CEO (managing partner), the chairman of the board, and the CEO's "kitchen cabinet" (a few lawyer, administrative, and support staff representatives). The number of people you involve at this early stage depends on several factors individual to your firm, including its size and management structure.

During our strategy sessions each member of the group learned what his or her role was in implementing different aspects of the plan and set about it without compromise. It is impossible to exaggerate the importance of building a strong core group that is "responsible" for developing the hows, whys, and whens of any plan for change and then carrying out the plan—the most obvious, and most difficult, part.

Identifying the Obstacles

Our first challenge was to anticipate as many obstacles as possible and strategize around or through them.

Lawyers generally function in a world of short-term goals; success is measured on a case-by-case or file-by-file basis. Being good lawyers, their strength, requires them to focus primarily on the immediate needs of their current files. Strategic long-term planning on business issues is secondary at best. Managing, and anything related to it, is considered anathema by most lawyers. This is a common situation in law firms, and the problem is routinely solved by relegating the long-term issues to a few "managing" lawyers and the administrative staff. The support staff probably functions even more than the lawyers in terms of short-term goals: completing the current backlog of dictation tapes, billing time entries, filing. It was critical that we understood and accepted this as a given: Do not expect immediate appreciation for your long-term goals. The greatest part of our firm was apt to see our "Excellence in Action" plan only in terms of what was happening immediately. In fact, we found that our greatest challenge was to keep our eyes on our long-term goals amidst all the angst and hoopla surrounding every small incremental change we made.

Expect resistance and skepticism! Jack Welch, CEO of General Electric, was successful in changing a huge organization that supposedly was incapable of change. He observed that "Change has no constituency"[2]; therefore, recognize that it will take time to build consensus for change, but it must be driven by the leaders of the organization. In the short term, do not measure your program's success by whether it is immediately accepted. Keep your eye on your long-term goals, and measure your success against them. In turn, a thorough strategy must include ways to measure the changes incrementally. We discuss this idea of objectively measuring your success in more detail later in this chapter.

Although we felt our strategy anticipated most problems, we were way off base on the amount of communication it would take to support such widespread changes in an organization. Chapter 6 discusses this issue in detail, but a good rule of thumb is that you will never be "finished" communicating. You must say the same things over and over. You must say them simply and consistently. And you must say them to everyone. With each new change, you must explain your long-term goals and how the current change fits with them.

Know Your Audiences

As you develop your strategy, you must determine what changes need to be made, identify your different audiences and their roles in the organization, and determine how the changes will affect them. This is not simply dividing your audience into lawyers and support staff. It means tailoring your communications to lawyers even further, because they may have different roles in and of themselves. They are, of course, lawyers handling files for their clients; but they can also be "leaders" of the firm, "managers" of their offices, "rainmakers" in client development, "learners" of new skills, and "team members" in their section or group.

The roles within the support staff encompass even more variations. You have the very obvious divisions in job titles: secretary, paralegal, billing clerk, accounting clerk, mail room personnel, information systems personnel, and so forth. Within each of those positions, there may be different roles, including "managers," "learners," and "team members."

Your audience and their roles may be defined even further by virtue of specific situations or circumstances that apply to them. For example, when attorneys are in a shared secretarial situation (two to one or three to two), you have an even more specific audience by virtue of the specific demands placed on those participants. We mention this because going to a shared situation represented a monumental change in our culture and brought with it many specific problems and solutions.

You must identify how your long-term goals involve and affect each of these groups and their many different roles. At the same time, you must deliver the same message to all audiences. You may have to say it differently, but the message must be consistent. Uniformity across all levels of the organization is an important foundation of effective change.

Build a Foundation for Change

To be successful, develop your strategy for change as concretely as possible. Begin with common underlying principles to give you guidance as you meet the never-ending challenges of change. Our plan for change, EIA, embodied a number of fundamental principles.

The "Cornerstones" of Excellence in Action:
- Share a common mission and focus
- Establish and teach quality standards and skills
- Support substantive continuing legal education
- Mentor, monitor, and measure results
- Reward quality performance
- Redefine quality service
- Build leadership and teamwork
- Use technology to improve quality

Additionally, we committed to the idea that every aspect of our plan had to touch every person at every level in the organization. These core principles became the foundation and the measurement for every change we made.

Share a Common Mission and Focus—What do you want to accomplish and why? State it simply and clearly and in a way that everyone understands. Make it visible and clear throughout the organization and refer to it constantly. In our firm, "Excellence in Action" said it all. For us, it meant the ongoing pursuit of quality for our clients. The adoption of this motto was an essential part of establishing a common mission and focus throughout our entire firm quickly. It was a simple statement calling for the highest level of performance with action now and in the future. We referenced "EIA" in internal communications, training materials, performance appraisals, etc., and were able to introduce and link what would otherwise appear as unrelated activities to a common goal.

Establish and Teach Quality Standards and Skills—A major emphasis of EIA was training, discussed in detail in Chapter 8. The framework of our ongoing training included the following guideline: Quality standards are defined by clients and employees. This meant that we had to learn a new communication tool: listening. We turned to our clients and our employees and asked them for ideas and suggestions on ways to improve.

Before we began teaching any classes, we distributed surveys and held a series of small meetings or focus groups. We asked our employees (lawyers and professional support staff) in these surveys and meetings to help us identify problem areas and to offer suggestions on firmwide quality standards. Through these focus groups and surveys, we incorporated the "best" of what we heard into our standards and communicated those new standards to everyone through our training classes and follow-up communications. Additionally, we also surveyed for those technical skills that were needed by each audience to do its job most efficiently and included them in our training program.

Support Substantive Continuing Legal Education—The Client Satisfaction Survey did not reveal problems in the area of technical expertise, but we decided that we needed to revitalize our in-house continuing legal education program, and we needed to continue to support our employees in carefully selected seminars and programs outside the firm. We suspect that client surveys across the country will reveal similar results. Do not ignore the technical competence issues, even though it is not competency that clients are complaining about, it's the service. Support for continuing legal education must be ongoing.

Mentor, Monitor, and Measure Results—Remember this important maxim: "What gets measured gets produced."[3] If you want a change to succeed, you must first determine what success means. That's harder than it sounds. Part of our strategy for change was the requirement that success be measured quantitatively. You must spend the time beforehand to determine how to measure your success: specific behavior changes, elimination of unnecessary steps, greater productivity, fewer write-offs, increased client satisfaction, improved morale, and so forth. You must determine how each one of your success factors can be measured. If you can't measure it, go back to the drawing board and spend more time identifying what you are trying to do and why. Once you determine how to measure your results, communicate your expectations clearly to everyone. Don't set people up for failure by making your goals a mystery. Make everyone's success at achieving their goals part of the firm's success.

The very fact that you are measuring requires that you pay attention to it—that you monitor it. The process of monitoring, however, is constant, while measurement occurs only at certain periodic intervals. The amount of attention you pay to a goal will directly influence the importance the organization places on it. Never introduce a change and then ignore its progress. You can be assured that it will fail.

We added another twist to monitoring at our firm and found it extremely valuable: peer review. We had peers share in monitoring the results of certain programs to determine whether the organization was achieving its stated goals. If we were falling short, we looked to them for ideas and suggestions on ways to improve. Initially, the idea of sharing responsibility for achieving the firm's goals was an alien concept to most. It led eventually, however, to an increased sense of "ownership" of the firm's goals.

The third part of this principle is the concept of supplementing formal training programs with mentoring. It is through mentor programs that the firm's standards and guidelines become personalized. Chapter 7 gives more information on mentoring.

Reward Quality Performance—We thought that rewarding would be the easiest principle to apply; we learned otherwise. Initial attempts at short-term employee recognition and reward were met with skepticism. We found that many employees felt that we had hidden motives in wanting to recognize and reward them for quality performance. You must realize that even positive change is hard for many to accept.

Your first step is to state clearly and consistently what you define as *quality performance*. This may require a revamping of your performance appraisal system. You must then provide whatever support and training is necessary to help employees achieve the standards. Rewarding quality performance can occur in a number of ways. Tie salary increases and year-end bonuses to clearly stated expectations. We also established employee award programs that recognize more than twenty employees a month. The recipients are nominated by their peers.

Redefine Quality Service—Make no mistake about it, the move toward TQM in our firm was client driven and it was specific. As we discussed in Chapter 1, the rules were changing in the legal services business. Clients determined what quality service meant to them and our job was to listen closely and deliver. In some instances, the quality of the legal work you perform may be secondary to the fact, for example, that your billing system is inconsistent and unreliable. The turnaround time of file handling may be more important for some clients than the outcome of individual matters.

In Chapter 1, we said that the best way to know what your clients want is to ask them. However, the process you use to ask is critical to what you learn. Spend the time (and money) to do it right. We found the formal Client Satisfaction Survey well worth the investment because it put us in a better position to deliver "quality service" the way the client wanted it. Conducting a client survey is not enough. You must analyze the results, incorporate them in your future training, and build a system to continuously measure yourself against your clients' standards.

Build Leadership and Teamwork—Leaders are often seen as a select few in an organization. Certainly, those in the position to determine the future of an organization must have leadership skills, but we believe that, in addition, every lawyer who works with a secretary or other support staff member must also know how to lead. And all managers and supervisors must possess leadership skills to do their jobs well. In the final analysis, everyone must have self-leadership skills.

At our firm, we prefer to speak of *leadership skills* rather than *management skills*. For some of you, the terms may be synonymous; for us there is a difference. It is sufficient at this point to state that for us, the principle of leadership affects everyone in an organization. An important emphasis of our plan was to define and communicate leadership expectations at every level in our firm, and then to teach those leadership skills. We felt that it was important that everyone "was singing out of the same hymnal." We researched and selected a leadership and development program that allowed us to share a common language of leadership expectations throughout the firm. It is called Situational Leadership II.[4] Our emphasis on building leadership skills is discussed in chapters 7 and 8.

Some law firms and organizations have built their culture on the team, or group, culture. Ours was not one of them. Heading into this program, we found that many of our lawyers operated as lone practitioners or "cowboys" under one roof. This sense of separateness was felt down through the secretarial ranks and into the administrative departments. We believed, however, that the future of our firm depended on a move away from this "cowboy" culture and into one of shared goals.

In a practical sense, the burden on the organization to do more with less personnel without compromising quality required more cooperation. We also knew that many of our future solutions had to come from the ranks of lawyers and support staff—the board of directors and CEO could not find and mandate every solution to every problem, and they certainly could not safeguard client service at every desk. The lack of teamwork skills in our organization was obvious, and strong medicine was in order. We researched and decided to build our teamwork program on the same model as our leadership program—Situational Leadership II.

Use Technology to Improve Quality—With the advent of technology and its associated high costs, many law firms set about to find a way to recoup those costs from clients. Word and data processing were seen as necessary evils, the cost of doing business in the 1980s. Any other use of computers was severely limited to those opportunities that could generate income or recoup the costs from the clients. In the midst of this, we did an unusual thing. We determined early on that technology should be used to enhance client service without any additional charge to our clients. We were not completely altruistic, however. We believed that the differentiation and competitive edge that technology could give us in attracting new clients and satisfying our current ones would more than make up for our costs.

We invested heavily in technology, in both people and equipment. Our emphasis and enthusiasm for technology came from how we used it to improve client service, efficiency, and productivity. We used technology in marketing our firm, using graphic and presentation software; we used it to keep our clients up to date through direct on-line access to our system; we used it as an extension of our firm's collective knowledge in our case management, expert witness, practice development, and work product systems. We saw a direct link between fewer people doing more and the use of powerful technological tools. Chapter 9 is devoted to an in-depth discussion of our use of technology in our TQM plan, but suffice it to say here that we see it as a critical piece of the program.

Developing Your Timetable

Your strategy should not consist of only lofty principles and goals. Each and every goal must be broken down to the individual steps required to accomplish it. Each step then becomes defined in terms of the master program timetable. Goals in one program will affect another program and should be timed accordingly. Develop both a timetable of what you want to accomplish on a yearly basis for at least the next two years and a detailed month-by-month schedule of goals, programs, dates of implementation, and responsibilities.

You will find that it is easy to be enthused and committed at the beginning of a program with all its associated attention. The danger lies in the implementation, when you have to keep moving forward a step at a time, even though the focus has shifted and the end still seems a long way off. The skeptics and dissenters are hovering at your door. The strength of your long-term goals will prevail only as long as you continue to communicate them again and again.

True change does not occur in the beginning of a plan for change. Initially, you may force a new way of doing things, but we can assure you that portions of your audiences will be quietly waiting for you to lose steam. They may remember all the "new" programs in the past, and how temporary they were. If you say something is scheduled to happen, make sure it happens. If the timetable changes, and it might, make sure you communicate loud and clear the reasons for the change. Never give the impression that you have "forgotten" a stated goal, program, or event. You must stay committed to your timetable and goals, month by month, week by week, even day by day. It is only through this persistence that your audiences will eventually adopt the changes and goals as their own. Change requires a tremendous amount of energy and enthusiasm. No one wants to spend that energy on a temporary fad. Your success depends on your commitment to each small step along the way.

What was the result of all our planning? We developed an action plan that had concrete steps. The only question that remained was When and how do we reveal the plan?

This is probably a good time to remind the reader that our suggestions for implementing a successful total quality program are based on our experience. That means that we learned from our mistakes. We did not do it right the first time, every time. In fact, we suffered through some slumps in our program when we got sidetracked on short-term problems and temporarily strayed from our timetable. We found that it took a lot more energy to restart a program than if we had kept to the promised timetable all along. You can generally assume that if we give you a warning or suggestion on how to implement your program, it's something that we learned the hard way.

Making It All Happen

1. Identify change agents who will commit and stay committed. This core group should be visionary in their thinking, in addition to being committed and creative. Support them, because they will be tested.

2. Educate your change agents about total quality.

3. Resolve that you will take calculated risks.

4. Meet with the firm leaders to identify barriers and obstacles to change and quality. Communicate your way around and through the organization in a simple, clear, and concise way.

5. With the information developed, Making It All Happen, at the end of Chapter 1, develop your plan, which in our view should include at a minimum the following:

   The "Cornerstones" of Excellence in Action:
   - Share a common mission and focus
   - Establish and teach quality standards and skills
   - Support substantive continuing legal education
   - Mentor, monitor, and measure results
   - Reward quality performance
   - Redefine quality service
   - Build leadership and teamwork
   - Use technology to improve quality

6. Develop and establish a timetable. Be flexible, but at the same time don't veer too far off the charted course. Remember, you will be tested, so get ready.

Chapter 3

Leading the Charge

Lawyers are really a conservative bunch. Even the most liberal minded and free thinking—the ones who consciously test the outer edges of the legal envelope (all, we might add, to the greater benefit of society)—nevertheless become comatose at the thought of change or disruption in their own firms. When two or more lawyers begin to associate together in firms, their interaction and the resulting management or leadership dynamic sometimes equals pure catatonia. If these thoughts are at all true (we will admit to some measure of hyperbole), a champion for change is a heretic, and a movement by more than one is an insurrection.

A less dramatic analysis, one you might more readily identify with, is that law firms generally are hierarchical organizations whose founders were entrepreneurial, although they didn't identify themselves in that way. Their past successes would understandably convince them that they should continue about their business in the usual way. How often have we heard "If it ain't broke, don't fix it." A corollary to that premise might be "If we are going to change, it had better be good."

Fortunately, in our organization we were blessed with senior lawyers who were open and flexible thinkers in spite of natural caution and skepticism. They recognized the need for change and were receptive to a plan for change, but the timing had to be right and, most of all, it had to be *valuable* change, something that truly would make a difference in our quality and thus improve our service to clients.

Presenting the Strategy for Change

Presenting the change to achieve the hoped-for success needed a well-thought-out, attention-grabbing presentation: "Look out, Baby, 'cause here we come." It needed to be communicated universally, to all offices, all practice groups, at the same time, in a visible, concrete way. A brainstorming session with the creative types in our training department suggested that first and foremost we needed the firm's leadership, the members of the board of directors, to see that the old way of doing things was going to have to go. We understood that we basically had one shot. If we were not able to persuade them of the need for change, we were unlikely to have another chance. We also realized that how we presented

So fee fi fo fum

Look out Baby 'cause here I come.

And I'm bringing you a love that's true

so get ready, So get ready.

I'm gonna try to make you love me too

so get ready, So get ready

here I come.

I'm on my way.

"Get Ready"
—The Temptations

our strategy and plan was an essential element of how it would be regarded. We developed the following theme:

There are vestiges of the Latin language still present in the law today. We thought that the board of directors surely would appreciate that this ancient language was not as useful as it once had been. "Omnia mutantur, nos et mutamur in illis," was a Latin saying that came to mind. The translation: "All things are changing, and we are changing with them." This was a thought we hoped we could convey.

Therefore, in a formal presentation to the board of directors we suggested that the once useful Latin language had had its day, but like many other good and useful things of the past, it must now give way to a new way of doing things.

We selected key words and phrases, translated the English terms to Latin, and used them as a springboard for presenting our strategy for change—the Excellence in Action (EIA) program. The actual presentation itself was prepared with computer graphics, and a presentation program was generated directly from the computer onto a large screen. (A representative highlight of the slides is included as Appendix E.) Through this presentation and the resulting discussions, we were able to obtain consensus and support from the firm leaders for our strategy.

This was only the beginning, however. Now we had the rest of the firm to persuade. The firmwide audience was very different. The remaining lawyers and support staff did not share the same responsibility of "guiding the firm into the future." They were more concerned with how a change or new program would disrupt their life, add more work, or "hurt" them in one way or another. They had heard the words "fewer people doing more" more times than they wanted to count. They had survived some hard times. Skepticism and morale problems were commonplace. They wanted things to be "like they used to be"—not more unpredictable change. We knew that a presentation would not be enough. It would take time—a long time—to convince everyone of the integrity of EIA and its goals. But we had to get the word out so we could begin.

The same presentation made to the firm's leaders was given to everyone. However, our emphasis in the firmwide meetings was not only on the goals of the EIA program but also on what it would mean to them: what changes they would see; what programs they would be asked to participate in; how the programs were related to each other and to the common goals of EIA. We wanted to dispel any notion that the EIA program was a collection of disparate, unrelated programs.

We introduced the EIA training program and schedule and its associated development of firmwide standards and guidelines. We announced the mentor program and planned revisions to the performance appraisal processes. We announced new technological tools that were in development and described how they would enhance efficiency and client service. We discussed the need to listen to our clients through a client survey and redefine client service to better meet their expectations. We presented the need for internal quality control through peer review and quality assurance programs. And we presented our plan for improved employee recognition and rewards for quality work.

They listened, applauded politely, and went back to their desks and offices, doubting whether any of these things would ever come to pass. The real challenge was ahead. We had to gain trust that what we promised would, in fact, occur. Things had to begin to happen and happen fast. The program had to have a visible impact on the organization; there could be no room for speculation or doubt as to the firm's commitment to this program.

Refer to the slides in Appendix E. Tailoring them to your firm as an illustration for an initial presentation may be helpful for you. With them, we were successful in grabbing the attention of all levels of the firm. There were many questions raised by the presentation, but the strategy for change in our firm was revealed for all to see. We established a common theme and focus, Excellence in Action, and a clearly defined plan.

Now, you may be asking yourself, How do I lead the charge? Educate your organization, if that is still necessary, about today's legal services marketplace. Redefine client service as clients do, not as lawyers do. Commit to developing an action plan. Be bold, creative, and innovative in presenting the strategy for change in your organization. That will get attention and will prepare the entire organization for a new, exciting journey.

Remember, much of what happens in life is affected by timing, by being in the right place at the right time. Remember also, you can wait for change or you can cause good timing and create change by being a leader and change agent. Look at the same old things in a new way. You can "Make It All Happen." Expect criticism along the way, but don't take it personally. In the end, lead.

The Door is Opened

One might inquire, who opened the door to all this change in our organization? What lawyers saw the problems and caused change? Were they visionary leaders of the firm's future?

The truth of the matter is that the knowledge that change was necessary came from the front-line troops. But, you might ask, is that not the lawyers (surely the associates)? No, if you really want to know why and where and how change is needed, ask those who are closest to the client. Unfortunately, the interaction between the lawyer and client can be formalistic and structured, so ask the members of your support staff what is needed.

Thieves in the night know that if you can crack open a door, even just a little, it's just a matter of time before you can walk right in. We needed an opening to have the run of the house. It was supplied by our support staff. Fortunately, our turnover rate was very low. It wasn't always the case, but during the time we were positioning the firm for change, we had tremendous stability at the support staff level and a strong commitment by most for improvement.

The fact that the front-line producers could most easily tell where the breakdowns were or would be, helped us immensely here. It was anecdotal evidence accumulated over a number of years, 1987 through 1990, together with attempts at little fixes to little islands of trouble, that convinced us that only a firmwide, top-down, bottom-up, all-encompassing program would solve the problem of constant energy spent on little fixes without long-term results.

During this time, we stayed close to the support staff, we listened and planned. We asked for and received an even stronger commitment, now that the opening of the door was getting wider and wider. There were times of self doubt, the usual amount of skepticism, but all in all, we were seeing it happen.

Total quality, however, needs to involve the entire organization. Now, with the backing of the firm's leadership and with the firmwide presentation completed, we needed to create momentum. Get ready, because here we come.

Making It All Happen

Think about the elements of a total quality plan that are needed for your organization, then:

1. Study the sample presentation slides in Appendix E again. They can be used to present your strategy for change. With a little creativity, you undoubtedly can come up with an attention-grabbing presentation that is right for your organization.

2. Remember that your organization will give the same credibility and weight to what you are presenting that you do. A sense of commitment, seriousness of purpose, and value must come through.

3. Don't move ahead unless you have some backing of the firm's leaders. Not all the ducks must be lined up in a row, but don't go it alone.

4. Don't be afraid to rummage around in some of the most unlikely spots in your firm for ideas, support, and commitment. We found it right under our noses. You may, too.

Chapter 4

Creating Momentum: Involving the Entire Organization

The word was out, something new was coming, but how could we create momentum for revolutionary change that cannot help but touch each member of the firm? The solution: more attention grabbing. This time, however, we developed a kickoff campaign, again involving all levels of the firm. Everyone knew, from the firmwide meeting, that something was in the works, but were they serious about change? Was this going to be just another program: quick to start and soon forgotten?

If we were going to combat some of the negative attitudes, we were convinced that the campaign needed to be novel, unique, and highly visible (hard to do in a conservative law firm atmosphere); focused on a theme; and constantly reinforced. The approach had to be something not seen in the firm before, nor could it be "traditional."

A little bit of history is in order here. In 1988, in anticipation of our celebration of 75 years of providing legal services, we shortened the firm name and developed a logo.

For our total quality process, we wanted a new logo that would incorporate our history, yet clearly communicate that something new was happening. We decided to call it "Excellence in Action." With the help of our communication consultants, we created a new logo.

Like a snowball rolling down the side of a snow covered hill,

Like the size of the fish that the man claims broke his reel.

Like the rosebud blooming in the warmth of the summer sun.

Like the tale by the time it's been told by more than one...

Every day it grows a little more than it was the day before...

And where it's gonna stop I'm sure nobody knows.

"It's Growing"
—The Temptations

We wanted the sense of a new direction and a change of pace, thus the high-tech-looking runner in full stride moving ahead, plus a statement about teamwork. Placing the EIA name in the bar provided the historical connection.

With the logo completed, we developed our campaign strategy. We built anticipation of the program with a postcard mailing to everyone announcing that "A New Team Is in Town." Over the weekend prior to the kickoff, we transformed the face of the firm with posters, balloons, coffee mugs and pins, all bearing the EIA logo. The same transformation took place in all of our branch offices. When our employees came to work on Monday, they were met with a "celebration"—we even had a jazz band in our lobby. The firm leaders met everyone personally, shook their hands, and welcomed them to "Excellence in Action." Fortune cookies predicting a great future were delivered to everyone that afternoon.

There were some dissenters and skeptics; more on that in Chapter 5. Generally speaking, it was a hit. We accomplished our goal. Everyone was talking about EIA. Some of the lawyers were overwhelmed. That is to say, they were taken aback because this, after all, was not what a traditional law firm was expected to do. Despite some negative reaction from the employees, in short order everyone was talking about EIA.

What about all of the hoopla? Some commentators have questioned the value of kickoff campaigns with a lot of whistles and bells, and others suggest that they have value but you should proceed with caution. Because of the very nature of the law firm, we thought it was important to shake things up a bit. A firmwide announcement or proclamation from the CEO would not have resulted in the immediate awareness that we sought and that our campaign accomplished.

In the ensuing months, EIA became an accepted theme. It was talked about daily and was visible everywhere. So we did not let up.

*This logo and the words Excellence in Action are claimed as service marks by Plunkett & Cooney, P.C.

At this point, the entire organization was on notice of EIA. Now, the question was how to involve them intimately in the plan.

For us, it was more focus groups (again at all levels of the firm). We wanted to find what was "best" practice in our organization. We knew that there was quality in what we did, but it was not universal. We needed to make quality available to every client at every engagement. We needed to be "easier to do business with"—all the time.

Before we began to teach any classes, we circulated surveys to our lawyers and professional support staff. We asked them to identify problem areas and to offer us suggestions on "best" practices and firmwide standards. We followed up these surveys with a series of small meetings or focus groups where the problems and suggestions identified in the surveys were discussed. These focus groups and standards surveys provided the information we needed and became the foundation for our EIA classes on quality practices.

The Problem of Measurement

Before we go any farther, we must comment on benchmarking. It is at this time in our program that it hit us again. "What gets measured gets produced."[1] To measure, you need a reference point. In TQM jargon, this is known as a *benchmark*.

For most people, pictures of assembly lines making widgets or accountants with green eyeshades toiling over ledger books probably come to mind. In the legal profession, lawyers are used to measuring in terms of numbers of cases or clients, in billable hours, or in cases won and lost. These "products" or outcomes are easy to quantify and measure. There is little ambiguity in interpreting the results. But when we talk about measuring quality improvements, assessing client service, and changing behavior and attitudes, the measurement tools, outcomes, and "products" are not quite as easy to quantify. This difficulty of choosing the right tools for quantifying what you are trying to measure often results in giving up and not measuring at all.

We know that measurement of client satisfaction with legal services is not as easily susceptible, at least at this point, to quantification by empirical data as is customer satisfaction in the manufacturing sector, which is measured, for example, in defects, cycle times, or customer retention. In the service industries, like Federal Express or UPS, on-time deliveries can be measured. The legal services industry does not have many published benchmarks readily available for comparison with best practices. How do law firms select "data and information for competitive comparisons?"[2] Who is "best in class" among law firms? For years, statistics about law firm performance consisted primarily of statements regarding

1. the number of employees in the firm (most often measured by the total number of lawyers in the firm)

2. a listing of major clients
3. starting salaries for new lawyers
4. gross income
5. revenue per partner

But where are the statistics on quality? Is there a benchmark for what is an acceptable realization rate for work billed (i.e., the difference between what a lawyer charges for his or her time and what he or she actually receives vs. the outcome of the matter)? What is an acceptable level of accounts receivable write-off? What about "cycle times" (i.e., how long a matter is open)? What is the standard? Clients will tell you the longer a matter is in the lawyer's office the higher the fees will be. Where are the statistics on this? In short, the profession needs to become infinitely more sophisticated in its measurement techniques, but that study will be the subject of a different endeavor.

It is simply important to note here that the value of any program to the organization will be quickly determined by whether anyone is paying attention to the results. Many organizations understand this to mean drawing attention to who's not doing the right thing. This may be essential when there is a lot of "testing" going on—i.e., "how serious are they about this?" But what is important is recognizing and building your core of champions and acknowledging those people who have demonstrated commitment to your program or goals.

There are several different elements to consider when you measure your results. The first is to determine what change you are looking for: Is it a definable action or behavior? Is it a less definable change in attitude? Is it an increase in participation by everyone or by a certain group? Is it an increase in profits, billable hours, or an expanded client base? Is it an increase in client satisfaction? Each of your quality programs is probably designed to have an impact on at least one of these, so spend some time defining quantifiable goals for each program or process. Each of these can be measured, but the means you use may differ.

Before you can measure results, however, you must determine your starting point. If you don't know where you were when you began, how will you know if your results are better or worse?

With thoughts of measurement in mind, we returned to strategizing our firmwide plan. We knew that success would only be obtained if the plan involved the entire organization. If you start small, your gains will be small. Your improvement will not be as perceptible as it will be if all are required to change. Improvement is hard enough to identify, quantify, and amplify; therefore, we started big, and are glad we did. Anything short of a firmwide effort would have lengthened the timeline for implementation way beyond acceptability. Some commentators on quality say start small, then "scale up." We think you should start big and "scale up." If you do, you can reach greater heights. It's riskier and more challenging, but the rewards will be greater.

Building Momentum

Because there is great risk in involving the entire organization rather than starting in a small practice group or department, responsibility for revolutionary change must necessarily be handled by the firm's leaders. At this point, your change agents must have done their thing—learning, planning, communicating—to raise the collective commitment of the firm's leaders. Once the firm's leaders are moving forward, you are on your way; success will not be just around the corner, it will be within sight.

The presentation to the board of directors had been a success. The kickoff campaign had been a success. We were on a roll. We might have been tempted to quit while we were ahead. We had discovered it was fun to start something new when it held such great promise, that the fanfare and the excitement were gratifying in and of themselves. We also knew, however, that we hadn't really even begun to achieve the goals of EIA. Achieving those goals would require us to pay as much attention to every detail of every promised program as we had to the presentation and kickoff campaign. It was apparent that the real momentum of change in our organization would occur only when everyone trusted the program and its promises, when they saw the impact of EIA on their everyday jobs, when they saw "total quality" results that gave them feelings of pride in ownership of the goals of the program, and most important, when clients began to notice that we were doing things better. Every cornerstone, every goal of the EIA program had to become visible and have an impact on every level in the organization in concrete ways in the first few months.

The EIA presentation promised several interrelated programs, all sharing common goals and all working together to achieve the common mission of total quality and continuous improvement. It also promised that each audience in our organization would be affected. Delivering on these promises became both a strategic and a leadership challenge. In a few short months the following programs were begun:

- Focus Groups on Restructuring the Performance Appraisal Process for Support Staff
- Focus Groups on Developing Quality Standards and Guidelines
- Support Staff and Attorney "Standards" Classes
- Substantive Continuing Legal Education Classes
- Technology Skills Assessments and Training
- Quarterly Office Swap
- Employee Recognition Programs
- Attorney Mentoring Program
- Revised Attorney Performance Appraisal Tools
- Client Satisfaction Survey
- Ongoing Client Satisfaction Monitoring (i.e., End-of-Matter Report Cards)
- New Technology Tools
- Leadership and Teambuilding Training

The EIA training program was a very visible piece of the program on an everyday basis. Attendance at EIA classes and seminars was mandatory, which allowed us to ensure that standards, guidelines, and goals were consistently communicated. As a side benefit, this very process of making the classes mandatory resulted in high credibility for the program and increasing acceptance throughout the organization. Everyone attended at least one training class each month, and the goals and mission of EIA were continuously present in everyone's life—there was no escape. As we will discuss in Chapter 8, each training class built on the previous one, and all were rooted in common themes and a language of continuous quality improvement.

Another critically important element of the training program was its ability to serve as a springboard for other related quality initiatives. For example, one of the EIA training classes was on "Billing Guidelines and Procedures." It was initially designed as a way to teach the correct billing procedures. In preparing the course material with the focus groups and firm leaders, however, another entirely different process occurred. We decided to reexamine the total billing process and determine if there was a better way to do it. The door to continuous improvement had been opened.

Similarly, our class on "Client Service," which evolved out of the Client Satisfaction Survey, served as a springboard for some revolutionary thinking. The EIA cornerstone of measuring and monitoring results had by this time become an accepted standard. As a result, during discussions on preparation of the course content for the Client Service class, much thought and discussion was given to how we could effectively monitor and measure our client's satisfaction. The brainstorming resulted in a new procedure in which client expectations were more clearly detailed in the engagement letter when a new file was opened, and when the file was closed, an end-of-matter report card was reworked to measure our client's satisfaction. This idea has since become a standard in the way we monitor and measure our clients' satisfaction.

The momentum for change continued as each class topic caused the question "Is there a better way?" to be asked.

Employee Involvement

The real momentum toward quality improvement in an organization is built on each person's individual commitment to that goal. It is impossible to monitor whether all are doing their "best." You cannot dictate or force excellence. If the goals of our EIA program were seen as something external, issued through a series of quality commands and edicts, our results would surely be hampered. Employees' buy-in and participation depend a great deal on how much they feel that their ideas and concerns are sought out and considered. You cannot fake it. If you are not interested in hearing ideas and concerns from your employees, don't ask. Don't put everyone through an exercise in futility; the credibility of your program will be seriously damaged, and trust will be lost. If you do ask, then you must be willing to listen earnestly, without reservation, and be willing to incorporate what you hear into your program.

Although we maintain an "open door" policy in our firm that encourages our employees to discuss their ideas and concerns with key decision makers, we wanted to build a more structured channel for input into our EIA program. This approach took shape in the form of focus groups. *Focus groups* are teams of employees who are brought together, either voluntarily or on request, to provide input and ideas on specific topics. Focus groups are different from open forums or town meetings or committees. Open forums and town meetings can serve an important function in establishing lines of open communication. These meetings, however, do not generally serve as vehicles for problem solving or, ultimately, solutions. Focus groups, on the other hand, are built on a shared sense of responsibility: "Management" commits to using the suggestions and ideas the focus group decides on; and the focus group commits to finding solutions that are consistent with the goals and mission of the firm.

We used focus groups and teams regularly to help us achieve the goals of the EIA program. A few specific instances are worth mentioning. The first involves the revamping of our support staff performance appraisal process. As in many law firms, the support staff performance appraisal or job evaluation process was casual and inconsistent. Lawyers were asked in a memo to evaluate the performance of their secretaries. The responding memos usually were a few sentences in length and commonly used words or phrases such as "outstanding," "irreplaceable," "could not function without her," and so on. The memo usually ended with the request to "give him as much as possible." There were no clear standards or guidelines on what constituted outstanding work, much less what would be considered acceptable. Performance expectations were unclear and unevenly applied.

Additionally, up until this point year-end "bonus" awards were based solely on length of service with the firm. The goals of our EIA program required that we monitor, measure, and reward employees on quality, not longevity. This meant that we had to revamp our performance appraisal and reward process to meet these guidelines and this would potentially affect everyone's pocketbook.

We turned to our employees for help. Focus groups of secretaries and administrative staff were formed with the purpose of creating a new performance management (appraisal) tool and bonus compensation system. The results were outstanding. Armed with a thorough understanding of the firm's mission of quality client service, the focus groups created a tool that better measured skill, commitment, expertise, and effort. The bonus system was also revised to directly reward commitment to quality, as demonstrated in an employees' performance. The new process was immediately implemented and continues to serve as the foundation for performance management and reward of our support staff.

We also formed focus groups to identify needed standards and guidelines that should be included in the EIA schedule of classes. Each topic warranted its own group discussion, and many of the actual standards and recommendations that were taught in the classes originated in these groups.

Listening to employees, however, does not mean you must concede on unpopular programs. Our Quarterly Office Swap is a program in which once a quarter members of our support staff swap offices within their practice sections and work for other lawyers for the day. The goals of the office swap are threefold: (1) to monitor the standards that have been taught in the EIA classes by having the participants complete a questionnaire; (2) to build teamwork within the practice section and a better understanding of what others do in their jobs every day; and (3) to emphasize that all staff must accept their personal mission of quality client service, no matter where they are sitting or what they are doing that day.

This program met a tremendous amount of resistance. We were wreaking havoc with the "sacred" lawyer/secretary relationship. Many years had been spent in building "their" ways of doing things. Many secretaries felt loyal not to the firm, but to the lawyers for whom they had worked for so long. When we listened, we found that most concerns centered around two issues: a feeling of disruption in their work day—a lost day—and the professional challenge of whether they were "good" enough to succeed in the other office where "their" ways might not work.

We met in several small meetings with each practice section and explained again and again the reasons behind the office swap: monitoring standards, building teamwork, and improving client service. We listened to the concerns and complaints. We challenged ourselves and questioned whether the goals of the programs were worth the pain. We decided that painful as it was, its value was considerable, and it would continue as an essential part of the EIA program. We listened, we considered; but we were not reactive to every complaint or criticism. The lesson: If the goals and strategy of your program have been thoroughly developed, you will be able to listen freely to all ideas, concerns, and criticisms but then rely on your cornerstones to make your decisions.

Employee Recognition Programs

Stephen Covey's best-seller, *The Seven Habits of Highly Effective People*,[3] discusses the "scarcity vs. abundance mentality." He reflects that some people believe that there is a finite amount of recognition and attention (or love, in a personal sense) for which people have to fight and undermine each other—the *scarcity mentality*. Other people believe that there is more than enough recognition and appreciation for everyone and that they are free to share in each other's success rather than compete—*the abundance mentality*. In the management literature there is also a wealth of information and research on the intrinsic and extrinsic values and benefits of employee recognition programs.

One of the cornerstones of the EIA program is its promise to recognize and reward employees for their commitment to quality, teamwork, and client service. This promise took shape in a collection of employee recognition programs: Suggestion of the Month, EIA Employee of the Month, and Employees of the Month Program. One "EIA Employee of the Month" is also selected from firmwide nominations submitted through a balloting process. From these nominations, our board of directors selects an employee for his or her outstanding contribution in the prior month. A monthly award ceremony occurs in which the two employees receive a plaque and gift certificate presented by the president/CEO or a member of the board of directors, as well as applause and recognition from their fellow employees.

The Employee of the Month Program centers around the practice sections. Members of each section select an employee from the group that they wish to recognize for his or her contribution. The section, as a group, determines the basis on which to select an employee, the procedure, and the award ceremony. In addition to the employee recognition benefits, this program also allowed us to sow the seeds of teambuilding in a positive way. The sections had to learn and apply the skills of working as a group to make the decisions and selection on a monthly basis. Each section Employee of the Month receives an award, a gift certificate, and a personal congratulation card from the president of the firm. Additionally, every month the names of all the employees recognized in the sections or by the board of directors are front-page news in our firm publication.

As we pointed out earlier, there will be bumps in the road, so be prepared. One of the more humorous ones for us was a realization after a few months that the coffee mugs carrying the EIA logo were not "excellent." We started to receive reports that they were exploding when filled with hot liquid! Fortunately no one was hurt and we knew a good lawyer who got us a refund. It sure gave the skeptics and dissenters something to focus on and have fun with. Speaking of skeptics and dissenters, how do you handle them? Chapter 5 will help.

Making It All Happen

1. Consider getting professional communications help to create momentum for implementation of your plan for total quality.

2. Plan a party that involves the entire firm—surprise parties are even better.

3. Have fun.

4. Execute your plan; don't waiver. Follow-up with a visible concrete step in your plan soon after the announcement. If you don't, the loss of momentum will hurt your progress. Remember that the staff will place the same emphasis on your program that you do.

5. Consider "starting big".

6. Involving the entire organization is just that. Start out by listening. There is an old adage that says "Nature has given us two ears and one mouth so we can listen twice as much as we talk." Slow down, listen, and gather ideas.

7. Formally recognize the involvement of your employees.

8. Don't take everything too seriously. Be able to make fun of yourself.

9. Have more fun.

Chapter 5

The Greatest Challenge: Achieving Buy-In

We have quite dramatically described the introduction of total quality concepts into a law firm as a revolution. Recent world history records tales of bloody cultural revolutions, some successful, some failed. There are also revolutions that are less violent in action but no less significant in the political changes they bring about. For law firms, it is enough to say that when you begin your total quality program, the resulting changes will surely touch your culture and will also affect the governance and management philosophy of your organization. As a consequence, you must be prepared to accept the idea that how the quality revolution is perceived by your employees will affect your ability to get buy-in from them.

A review of the literature will detail many examples of how manufacturing companies have implemented Total Quality Management (TQM) in their organizations. Directly applying these findings to the law firm environment, however, can prove to be ill-advised. For example, one CEO of a small manufacturing company that was committed to a two-year total quality effort had several lessons he learned. One of them: Give your middle managers sufficient time to get with the program—if they don't, send them packing.

Such a lesson is not easily applied to law firms. The reason: Law firms are unique organizations. Unlike manufacturing concerns that may have layers and layers of management, each with separate roles, many of the people who must buy into the program in a law firm are not only your middle managers but also your sales force, your production supervisors, your workers (who also do a lot of their own accounting, that is, keep time, produce invoices, etc.), all rolled into one. They are the lawyers. Suffice it to say that law firms are unique organizations, and your revolutionary program has to be carefully planned so that you are successful within your own unique culture. As we have said repeatedly throughout this book, do not simply introduce a TQM concept or lesson without first carefully analyzing how it applies to law firms in general and to your organization in particular.

I can turn the gray sky bluer,

And I can make it rain whenever I want it to.

I can build a castle from a single grain of sand,

I can make a ship sail, yeah on dry land.

But my life is incomplete, and I'm so blue,

'cause I Can't Get Next To You.

"I Can't Get Next To You"
—The Temptations

No Guts, No Glory

Building a total quality program in a law firm is not for the faint of heart. You should not embark upon it lightly, for a failed quality initiative is worse than none at all. You probably won't get a second chance if you blow it the first time around. Change takes a tremendous amount of energy by every person. If you threaten change, put everyone through unnecessary turmoil, and then end up where you began, you will have lost the trust of the organization. And trust may be your strongest asset, especially through the first stages of your quality revolution.

So how do you ensure the success of a quality revolution and achieve buy-in? It helps to have your vision and goals clearly stated. It helps to have strong leaders and committed change agents. It helps to have well-thought-out programs and strategies. But total quality requires the commitment and involvement of every person in your organization.

You Can't Do It Alone—Those who study group dynamics will tell you that with any change experienced by a group, individuals will respond initially in one of three ways. There will be the early adopters, the skeptical majority, and the laggards. Knowing that there will be these three general responses to change, the question arises: How do you deal with them?

We knew that at one end of the spectrum there would be early adopters—the ones who are the first to jump on any bandwagon. They can be your salvation or your demise, depending on their reputation in your organization. If they are the leaders and can see the wisdom of your long-term goals and plans, they will be essential to building the momentum for change and persuading the skeptics. If these early adopters are perceived as kooks or radicals, then their support may hinder the general acceptance of your program. At the other end will be the laggards—the ones who will never be convinced and refuse to be a part of any change.

In the middle will be the skeptical majority—this is where your success or failure ultimately lies. This is where your army of heroes and role models will originate. And this is where you should target most of your energies. Focus your strategies on how you can help them through the change, and make them supporters of your quality revolution.

One tactic we used to further acceptance of our goals was to surround the questioning souls of the skeptical majority and the laggards with constant communication and friendly persuasion. It is a mistake to ignore or dismiss their questions and concerns. In fact, it's best to do just the opposite and encourage ongoing discussion of quality issues and goals. We found that circulating articles from current publications pertaining to our program with notes in the margin was a good way to start. "What do you think?" "Let's discuss." "Give me a call." We also suggest that your credibility will be enhanced if you include articles that are controversial from your point of view—those that may question the goals or strategies of your program. They can be a great source of open discussion. Nothing, however, is as effective as one-on-one discussions. Never pass up an opportunity to communicate the need for change or to discuss the whys and hows of your program. Your biggest enemy, of course, always will be time. In the scheme of things, however, time invested in constant communication with members of your organization will speed the process of acceptance.

No matter how hard you work at communication, there will be some that will not accept change. Over time, they will have to make their own decisions as to how long they will resist. But never give up on anyone; your program's success or failure can be measured one person at a time.

Building Your Army

As we observed earlier, the initial impetus for your quality revolution probably will come from a small group of committed change agents. You may be successful for a short period of time in moving the organization forward through a series of new programs and changes. In the beginning, the rush of activity caused by this new program may move people along by sheer momentum. At some point, however, people can fall off the wagon. They can find ways to circumvent, even sabotage, the program. If your change agents are seen as an isolated elite group, then your revolution may be overthrown by the old party-liners who are longing to return to the good old days, as foolish as that is in today's market.

You have to focus your strategy from the very beginning on building your army of role models. That is where the heart of your support will be. Your role models should be selected from the skeptical majority. They have the same questions and concerns as everyone else. They are not seen as joiners or loners, but they are the ones that your organization will look to for direction on how to act and feel through all the turmoil. They can interpret the quality goals in individual ways that make sense to them and to their peers, and act in relation to these goals in an everyday way. In fact, it's best that they don't preach the gospel directly from the sermon notes but say it in their own way, with their own words about their own feelings.

It is so easy when you are at the center of your quality revolution to believe that your goals and plans are clear to everyone. We found that months into our program, some people still didn't understand what "Excellence in Action" was all about. We talk about communication in other chapters, and it is certainly an essential part of clarifying your vision. But you also have to allow more and more people to make your vision their own and then let them explain it to their peers. Help the skeptical majority understand and adopt the vision.

Therefore, we see the greatest challenge for law firm leaders is gaining buy-in for the change process from the skeptical majority who go about their business in their usual fashion day in and day out. Know well that there will be not only dissenters and skeptics but also those who downright will not buy into the program at any cost. Their resistance does not make them bad people (in fact, they can be a good reality check on revolutionary thought and plans), nor are their thoughts and ideas necessarily wrong. But there is a danger that they may slow the process of acceptance and involvement too much if their criticisms gain enough credence.

It is not only the laggards who will demonstrate resistance to change. Depending on the extent of change involved, nearly everyone will resist at some point. How do you understand these dynamics of change and resistance and learn to manage them instead of only reacting to them?

How Do You Tell When You're Winning or Losing?

We spent many hours reviewing material on how people react to organizational change. We thought we were well prepared and knew what to expect. We were kidding ourselves. We found that we could not determine if we had succeeded or failed until we learned to ask and answer a few key questions: What kind of resistance and morale problems can you expect to be associated with change, including "good" change? What is the difference in the type or degree of resistance and morale problems that identify a serious failure of your program to gain commitment and acceptance? In many cases the answer is a matter of degree, time lapsed, and whom you're talking with.

The first rule is to expect resistance when new ideas or programs are introduced. Also, understand that any change or modification to an existing, accepted program will probably set a wave of resistance in motion. Allow several months to pass before measuring any level of success or failure. We have talked several times throughout this book about the necessity of developing concrete ways to measure success. If you have clearly identified what you want to accomplish with a program, you will be able to measure whether you have made any steps in achieving your goals. Don't expect to have complete consensus or success the first time around. Let a program continue through several measurement periods, then measure whether there is any evidence of progression. Learn to measure your success incrementally, one step at a time. On the other hand, don't be too proud to learn from your mistakes. If something isn't showing any evidence of success after several measurement periods have passed, fix it, change your approach, or if you can't fix it, drop it.

The second rule is to recognize whom you are listening to in determining your program's success or failure. The early adopters will make you feel good with their enthusiastic support, but you must be careful not to be lulled into false complacency by them. On the other hand, don't pay too much attention to the laggards and their constant expressions of impending doom. Depend on your cadre of skeptical majority representatives to give you a clear, accurate picture. They may not accept or like your program initially, but after a period of time has passed, they should be able to give you good guidance on its strengths and weaknesses.

Change Is Hard—Be careful not to measure the value or worth of your quality program and its goals by the amount of resistance it receives. The survival of your firm may be at stake, yet people will still resist the change. We thought we had all the answers but learned quickly, as Jack Welch simply stated, "Change has no constituency."[1]

In introducing the goals of our quality program, we thought that presenting compelling reasons for the change would be enough to convince almost everyone of the need for change: The legal marketplace is changing. Clients are more sophisticated in their choice and monitoring of counsel. Service-related issues had become more important to clients as technical legal competence becomes a given. Therefore, who could argue with a program whose focus is quality and client service, right? Wrong.

The program represented a substantial change from earlier practice. And change is hard, no matter how necessary the change may be. It is as simple as that, and also as complex. Almost everyone will ask What could I lose in this change process? They will not ask What could I gain? Depending on how much there is potentially to lose, you can expect a powerful forcefield of resistance. Do you blast through it? Do you go around it? Or can you convince everyone to lower his or her shield and get the buy-in you need? Before you can decide how to manage change in your organization, you must understand how and why people react to it so negatively.

Why People Resist Change—How people react to change has a lot to do with whether they feel they have any control over it. Most people need to feel that they have some control, some impact, on the events occurring around them: "Change is exciting when it is done by us, threatening when done to us."[2] This is what ownership, empowerment, and participative management is all about. As the well-known organizational behaviorist Rosabeth Moss Kanter states, "When people feel powerless, they behave in petty territorial ways."[3]

When people feel powerless to stop bad things happening all around them, they will look for someone or something to blame. We recognized that we had little or no control over the events in the changing marketplace or the increasing client demands and service expectations, and so a total quality initiative was begun in order to survive the chaotic market. However, the people in your organization may not recognize or appreciate these external events. The only change they see is close to home: this new program you've instituted. Thus, you run the risk that they may blame your total quality program for all the ill effects seen inside your firm, rather than acknowledging that the bad things outside the firm are the real culprits.

To increase a sense of control, it is important to involve more and more people in the decisions that affect their future. Involvement even in small details surrounding a new program or plan is better than total noninvolvement. As understanding and commitment increase, so should the shared responsibility for change. Making people a part of the solution is more than a pat phrase. It is vital.

Also, be careful that as you present your reasons for change you don't build your program on the assumption that the old ways were wrong. This will put all those who supported them in a defensive posture and can create only a win/lose environment. Put the new ways into perspective—we could not be where we are now without the benefits of our roots and history.

Developing Your Strategy for Change—We refer frequently to a few key books that helped us build our strategy for change. Two of these books, *Teaching the Elephant to Dance*,[4] and *The Leadership Challenge*,[5] discuss how to prepare and move an organization through change. They discuss similar key points, but each says it a little differently. We found both of these books very helpful in describing the effects of change and how to manage them.

What Is the Future?—If you want people to give up the security and predictability of the present, you must give them a reason to believe in a better future: ". . . an energizing, inspiring vision is the key to mobilizing support. This vision is the picture that drives all action."[6]

The picture you present of the future must be clear and must be seen as attainable. People want to be a part of something successful. If your vision is seen as something either far removed from everyone's experience or unattainable and you are unable to make it real to them, you will never gain acceptance. You must be able to describe vividly and in detail how your quality program will improve everyone's life, whether materially or otherwise. You must be able to enlist everyone, not only intellectually but also emotionally.

People relax when they believe that someone is in charge. They may complain or resist, but this is nothing like the raw panic you see in organizations when there is a void in direction and leadership. You must persuade your organization that you know where you're going, how you are going to get there, and what the future will be like. This is the job of the leader: "Leaders breathe life into visions. They communicate their hopes and dreams so that others clearly understand and accept them as their own."[5]

We have talked in earlier chapters about how you go about creating a firmwide common mission. We will talk more in Chapter 7 about the role of leadership in communicating this vision. Envisioning the future—creating your tomorrow—is an essential first step in the organizational change process. But having a vision is not enough. "The walls of most organizations are littered with the graffiti of too many visions. People must use your vision to make it real."[7]

Actions Speak Louder Than Words—Teach (and lead) by example. Demonstrate that the change you are promoting can be achieved. Threatened, unclear, or unknown change will paralyze your organization. Don't keep it a mystery. Talk about the change all the time, then demonstrate it. Show everyone by your actions what you expect from them. The leaders must set the stage, and the skeptical majority role models must be in the chorus. It is essential that your program and its goals show consistency between what is said and what is done. If the messages differ, you will confuse everyone with the inconsistency. Confusion is a serious obstacle to change.

Identify the actions or behaviors that are key to change. If you see even a glimpse of those positive behaviors in someone else, acknowledge it, reward it, and celebrate it in visible ways for the whole organization to see. This will increase the ranks of heroes, which are critical to growing acceptance of and support for your program. You need these heroes so that your organization can learn the winning ways by watching other winners. People will expect *you* to live your vision, but it is only when they see their respected peers begin to say what you say and do what you do that the change has really begun. It is at that point that they will begin to trust in the change and in the new future. Buy-in on a wide scale is now possible.

Build on Small Wins—Remember that every win counts. It is through the small victories that you build momentum. People want to be winners, and the next best thing to being a winner is to be associated with one. Brag about your wins. Celebrate the small victories. Your wins will get people to want to join in, to want to be a part of the success. The foundation of action is commitment. Once you get people to act, the vision and future is no longer yours, it is theirs. Each win builds people's confidence in and commitment to the vision and to the future. Each win makes it harder for those who want to return to the old ways to do so.

Expect It and Measure It, or Forget It—Here is another simple but important maxim to help you get buy-in: "If you don't expect it—and tell your people you want it—you'll never get it. People are very poor mind readers."[8] People are motivated when they can see and measure the outcome. Once you've set your expectations, don't waver. You will be tested. You will have to justify the whys and hows. If you're well prepared, your well-thought-out vision and strategic plans will let you easily answer any objections.

"What gets measured gets produced." We've talked a lot at different points in this book on the value of identifying what you want to achieve in ways you can measure. How will I know if I'm doing what I should? How will I know if I've achieved the goal? These are questions you must struggle with on an organizationwide basis. But these are also issues for every single person in your organization. You must give them the yardstick to measure their own successes. Provide the feedback as immediately as possible, and then at every incremental step on the climb toward improvement. Don't hide behind secrecy. If sharing information will increase commitment and responsibility, then share it. Don't keep the results of your measurements under lock and key if you need everyone's help to achieve your goals. Through this sharing you will get buy-in.

You've stated your expectations; you've measured the results. What do you do with this information? If what gets measured gets produced, then, just as important, "what gets rewarded, gets produced again."[9] Make your rewards highly visible when you are trying to motivate people to change. Rewarding the right behaviors will build momentum faster than any other tactic. Use many different rewards for those who demonstrate the vision. Money talks, but don't overemphasize its importance for long-term results. If used singly as a reward, it usually only reaps short-term benefits. On the other hand, don't ignore the message that an *unfair* monetary reward system sends. If people feel underpaid or underappreciated in comparison with others, they will not be motivated to change. If nothing else, make sure that your monetary reward system is based on fair, consistent criteria. Spread your rewards around. Don't be stingy—reward individuals and reward groups. Recognition and autonomy are powerful rewards.

Making It All Happen

1. To achieve buy-in to your program, find out who your dissenters and skeptics might be. Don't worry too much about having to identify them. You can probably list them now. Rest assured that at some point they will make themselves known.

2. If introducing a total quality program for your organization is revolutionary, recognize that change will be seen as an enemy. Lead and communicate to defeat the enemy.

3. Spend most of your time with the skeptical majority, but don't ignore the laggards. Communicate with them at every opportunity.

4. Share your vision, and celebrate even your small wins.

5. What gets measured, gets produced. Measure and monitor your leadership and the effectiveness of your communication by talking with everyone you can.

6. We hope you will have taken our earlier advice and built an army of change agents and role models. Remember you can't go it alone, so if you feel you are losing momentum or support, go back to Chapter 2 and reevaluate your plan. Start again if you have to.

Chapter 6

Communicating in New Ways; Sharing a Common Vision; Staying the Course

In Chapter 1 we suggested that as a result of focus groups and surveys you would gain an understanding of your client's goals and expectations to help you develop your action plan, as described in Chapter 2. You will use the information to implement the plan (chapters 3 and 4). Now you must ensure that the vision for the future that has grown out of all this effort is visible, clear, focused, and evident for all to see.

Sharing a Common Vision

What does everyone want to know? It is really quite simple. Remember your family trips or vacations. Most often, they were planned months in advance and around a specific person's vacation or a holiday. Thus, the family anticipated the upcoming event, and could look forward to it at a scheduled time.

Of course, there was thorough discussion about where the family was going and about the reasons for the destination (to see relatives? for rest and relaxation?). Your firm is no different. It is on a journey. But where? And for what reason? Once those decisions are made, the question becomes How will you get there? As the time for departure on your journey approaches, the questions of how, when, and why become more important. It is at this time that specific plans need to be revealed. Have you done that with your organization? Have you shared the vision? Are you specific?

mm I bet you're wonderin' how I knew

'bout your plans to make me blue...

It took me by surprise I must say

when I found out yesterday

don't you know that I heard it through the grapevine...

**"I Heard it Through the Grapevine"
—Gladys Knight and the Pips**

The Real Test

Let's assume that you've done everything right up until now. Your short- and long-term quality goals are clearly defined. You've developed the programs to help you achieve those goals. You've identified how you will measure your success in concrete ways. You've created enough attention and momentum to get the ball rolling. And you have worked through the initial resistance and find that your army of supporters is increasing.

How can you tell if you're on track in achieving your goals? We found that it is easy to assume success (or failure) if you measure only the results of each separate program individually. There is a danger in viewing your quality initiative as a series of separate programs rather than what it really is: a deep-seated change in your organization that goes to the very heart of how you do business.

The real evidence of success of any quality revolution is when its goals and concepts have so permeated the organization that employees begin to talk and act differently in the way they do their jobs. Quality and efficiency are no longer external goals monitored by supervisors, managers, and senior partners, but instead become self-monitored in every daily task. Employees are willing to challenge each other if they see poor quality or poor client service occurring. Employees begin to take great pride in responding more quickly to requests and doing more than the minimum to meet client demands. There is a greater sense of common purpose among all employees that transcends any lines of position or status. Everyone's role is seen as valuable in achieving quality goals and is demonstrated in increased initiative. You can visibly see employees openly sharing opinions and ideas with each other. Client service is no longer just the way we treat our outside clients, it is demonstrated in the way we treat each other in the organization.

Communicating in New Ways

How is this common vision established and maintained? We believe that communication—talking, listening, and demonstrating—is how the foundation is laid. This approach is difficult to employ, however, because most law firm cultures are based on a reticence toward "unnecessary" communication. If it is not billable or does not directly relate to a client (or compensation), communication is usually viewed as a frivolous and "bureaucratic" activity that should be kept to a minimum.

It is no wonder that lawyers hate memos and meetings. Time is considered every lawyer's enemy. In the "olden days" clients drove lawyers to become timekeepers because the clients wanted an objective measure of the lawyers' efforts other than a simple one-line bill for services rendered. Now, sophisticated time and billing programs have left no billable event unaccounted for.

This "quiet" law firm culture runs contrary to the flood of communication required to cause change in an organization. Is it possible to merge these two worlds? It's quite a challenge, but we found it could be done.

Keep it short—Keeping a lawyer at a nonbillable meeting for more than an hour is asking for bloodshed. Balance time with frequency. You will find greater acceptance of frequent communications when they are brief in duration. We held several firmwide meetings over a few months, but kept the length of each meeting to forty-five minutes. Be aware of the preferences of your different audiences when communicating. In scheduling our classes, we found much less resistance on the part of lawyers when we scheduled them for the evening or weekend. This tactic had the opposite effect with our support staff, however, who were much more supportive when their classes were held during the workday.

Build on your established structure—Our practice sections have always met on a monthly or bimonthly basis to discuss the status of cases and client development. We used those established structures to communicate with the lawyers by requesting fifteen-minute time slots during which we would present our program goals or specifics. With our support staff, we would often quietly invade the lunchroom during lunch periods or break times and begin discussions one-on-one or in groups. In addition, for many years our firm has distributed a weekly newsletter called the *Communicator;* we found that to be a valuable tool to share information about our quality programs on a firmwide basis.

Use formal and informal communication—Our CEO would report formally every month to our board of directors on our quality initiative, and this report was also distributed to the partners, in the form of minutes. He also met at least twice a month with every practice section leader in an informal meeting or at lunch; at this time our quality goals and programs always seemed to find their way into the conversation. Formal focus groups were established in which our support staff would investigate problems and suggest solutions. Informal brainstorming sessions were also held where we would simply ask employees to attend on short notice and offer their ideas and views on certain topics. Our "open door" policy became an important way to communicate, especially to listen, as everyone was encouraged to address individual questions and concerns about what we were trying to accomplish with the leaders of the firm.

Use a variety of communication tools—Use whatever resources you have on hand to communicate. We used E-mail, voice mail, written memos and newsletters, meetings, classes, and one-on-one discussions.

Be creative—If you communicate in the same old ways, your message will be perceived in the same old way. You must devise new ways of communicating. We used our Excellence in Action logo on posters, on meeting and classroom walls, and on most written documents discussing or related to our quality programs. We used computerized presentation software and desktop publishing to spice up presentations and written documents. We also used videotapes of known experts (e.g., Ken Blanchard, Tom Peters) in our presentations and classes to provide other perspectives. As we will discuss in more detail in Chapter 8, "The Role of Training," we avoided dry training presentations and used a variety of gimmicks and creative approaches.

Never let there be a void or vacuum of communication—If there is, it will fill up with rumors and misinformation—"don't you know, I heard it through the grapevine." The rule of thumb became communicate not once, not twice, but thrice.

This recommendation comes from another lesson we learned the hard way. At one point, our secretarial staffing concern reached a crisis stage. We were committed to reducing the lawyer/secretary ratio and, therefore, had not hired replacement secretaries for several months. We were heading into the summer vacation months, and it became obvious that without some staffing reorganization, many offices would simply be unstaffed for weeks at a time. Our section leaders took charge and helped solve the problem through restructuring the way their sections were staffed; they created shared teams and freed up several secretaries to act as "floaters" to cover absences and vacations. The good news was that the leadership was strong and evident. The bad news was that we did a very poor job of communicating the reasons for the change to the professional support staff. Many felt uprooted and displaced by the change. We had broken an important rule. No matter how critical the problem is, it is essential to make the time to communicate the reason for the change and discuss its effects on those involved.

Nothing is Sacred

"Workflow analysis" and "reengineered processes" are current hallmarks of TQM literature. What these concepts convey is quite simple: Reexamine every facet of the way you do business to identify areas of waste and poor-quality client service. This is the essence of total quality. When you have moved beyond slogans, meetings, and classes and actually begin to examine long-established business practices and procedures to improve quality, client service, and efficiency, you will have reached a critical quality watermark.

Once it is apparent to your organization that nothing is sacred when quality and client service are at stake, you will find that individual employees will follow suit and begin to examine their own private practices and procedures in terms of quality and efficiency.

We examined nearly every piece of our workflow in terms of how we could improve client service, quality, and efficiency, and found much room for improvement. Staffing, opening files, closing files, communicating with clients, consistency of quality in work product, billing process, technology, training—none was left untouched.

For example, we examined and dramatically changed our billing process with one clear focus: What did our clients want? How did they want their bills to look? What kinds of information did they want them to contain? How did they want to receive them (e.g., electronically)? We actually changed our billing codes (this is sacred turf) because they no longer served our clients' needs. It is almost beyond belief that we, a law firm, were willing to spend the time to reexamine and modify an internal process as protected as the billing system solely to meet our clients' changing needs. It was evident that a deep-seated change in the very heart of the way we did business had occurred.

We also changed our process of opening files to not only meet but exceed our clients' expectations. Our clients had told us through the client survey results that to them, one criterion of outstanding client service was faster and better communication. This included more frequent communication, up-to-date status reports, and thorough, yet concise, reporting. We reexamined our file opening process with the goal of improving our existing procedures to address these concerns. As a result, we made several significant changes. We modified our file-open timetable to ensure a minimum delay. We set a one-hour benchmark to open a file from client request to completion and built a new process around that benchmark. We revised our engagement letter to eliminate "legalese," and to discuss issues of concern to our clients beyond the standard fee structure or billing timetable sections. We standardized reporting procedures to guarantee that our clients received regular status reports on a set schedule during the early stages of a file: 7 days, 30 days, 60 to 90 days. For litigation matters, significant pleadings and status reports were hand-delivered and discussed face-to-face with clients, to ensure consensus on case-handling strategies and tactics, especially during the initial stages of a file.

In the same spirit of self-analysis, we also examined our file-closing procedure. One significant change that we made merits further discussion. We used the closing-files process to help us better measure our clients' satisfaction with us. All of the changes we made and, in fact, our entire quality initiative, would be for naught if it did not meet our clients' needs. Quality and client service is, purely and simply, what our clients say it is. We began to send end-of-matter report cards to our clients as each matter was closed. Several key questions concerning their satisfaction with us and our work were asked on a brief questionnaire. Their responses became the foundation for measuring our success in improving quality and client service. Any "less-than-satisfied" response from a client received a personal follow-up from a senior partner in our firm (president, director, or section leader).

Staying the Course

As more and more established procedures are examined and changed to improve client service and quality, the message will be loud and clear. Your quality program is not a passing fad or fancy. The organization and everyone in it are expected to change if quality, efficiency, or client service are at issue.

To maintain the course of a quality revolution in your law firm, a continuous movement toward improved quality and client service must be visible. However, every new change no longer has to be announced with horns blaring. Rather, the culture of "continuous improvement" will become seen as the "new" way of doing business.

Making It All Happen

1. Throw out the old ways of communicating.

2. Communicate not once, not twice, but thrice, with a constant and consistent theme.

3. Memorialize all you are doing for review purposes. A helter-skelter approach will just not do.

4. Give value to effective communication of nonclient matters by requiring formality.

5. Develop an in-house newsletter that is published on a regular basis.

6. Get a voice-mail system and use E-mail.

7. Appendix F has a standard agenda for practice groups or section or department meetings. From this you can build a trail of information for your business or marketing plan.

8. Call for commitment to the business or marketing plan. Make your leaders communicate the state of affairs. Knowledge is power, so energize your people to do more by communicating knowledge.

9. Communicate the identity and the nature of the work coming from new clients and old.

10. Use your new communications strategy to share your vision.

11. Stay the course.

Part Two

Evolution

The Role of Leadership

Plunkett & Cooney grew up as a so-called insurance defense firm. Founded in 1913 by Frederick Ward, the firm adjusted claim losses. Ward's cousin Robert Plunkett joined the firm and developed his reputation as a trial lawyer primarily with automobile negligence cases. William Patrick Cooney joined the firm in 1940, and led the firm after World War II. For one half of the firm's history, Cooney fulfilled the leadership role, his Irish wit and charm, his discipline, and his integrity making him the definitive benevolent dictator. He left us too soon in 1981. He was one in a million.

The litigation boom of the 1960s resulted in rapid growth in the firm business and lawyer head count. Robert Rutt, himself a legendary defense lawyer, eventually became the firm's first managing partner. Other firm leaders had been emerging for years. They too had vision and steered the ship through both troubled and calm waters which included a serious move to diversification in the late 1970s and early 1980s. The firm enjoyed growth. During the 1980s it became apparent that the firm was in need of more and more leaders who could take on practice area responsibility, committee assignments, and so forth. It became clear that many of our lawyers did not recognize, feel comfortable with, or execute the role of leader (manager) easily. What phenomenon was present here?

Most lawyers we know had highly successful academic careers, both in high school and in college, that gave them the opportunity to enter professional school, to excel there as well. They were leaders of their high school and college classes: involved young women and men who chose the legal profession, for the most part, because it was intellectually challenging. They had the ability, and they saw the representation of clients whose troubles would be laid at their doors as a noble and rewarding undertaking.

They did not go to law school to become actors, writers, teachers, social workers, salespersons, production supervisors, financial consultants, human resource managers, business managers, or politicians. Yet the practice of law today requires lawyers to possess skills and talents of each of these occupations and professions.

I'll sacrifice for you dedicate my life for you. I will go where you lead always there in time of need.

And when I lose my will you'll be there to push me up the hill

"You're All I Need to Get By"
—Marvin Gaye and Tammy Terrell

Once the Rule in Shelley's Case[1] has been memorized and forgotten, the graduate law students and new lawyers need to develop skills that allow them to offer clients or potential clients real-world answers that meet the clients' goals. Knowledge of those other skills, we believe, would serve them better.

In other words, most law schools do not offer nonlegal classes in

- Business organizations
- Government and government regulation
- Litigation management
- Investigation and information gathering
- Commercial transactions
- Effective oral and written communication
- Negotiation

Nor do they teach these other useful skills that help people lead:

- Leadership
- Management
- Professionalism and business ethics
- Problem solving
- Human resource management
- Team building
- Mentoring
- Effective public speaking
- Holding useful meetings

Lest this turn into an editorial for radically revamping law-school curriculums, one more observation. While the schools churned out more graduates versed in the Rule against Perpetuities and ready to tackle contingent remainders on the bar exam, the market could no longer absorb them as it had in the past. Our experience was that in-house legal staffs were growing, although the literature was reporting shrinkage in some places. We did learn that at least one leader of quality for in-house legal staffs was extolling the virtue of letting law firms train lawyers so they could be picked off just after they become productive but before they made partner. Remember that many general counsels were also outright complaining that they were not going to pay the expense (in the form of fees) for a law firm to educate their associates. In short form, what this meant is that law firms, not law schools, should train lawyers for useful work at the end of three or five or seven years, while absorbing the costs so that they can become productive as in-house lawyers. Now the editorial: Why don't we get into a win/win situation and have law schools train lawyers, followed by internship in law firms, courts, and corporate legal staffs? Thus the profession as a whole will have responsibility for training, and the cost can be more equitably spread around.

So much for the editorial. The role of leadership in the quality evolution that follows the revolution is key, but what is leadership and what is all the hoopla surrounding it in management circles all about?

Bookstores seem to be full of treatises and texts on leadership, including: *Leadership is an Art,*[2] by Max Depree; *On Becoming a Leader,*[3] by Warren Bennis; *The Leadership Challenge,*[4] by Kouzes and Posner; *Principle Centered Leadership,*[5] by Stephen Covey. Need a role model? There are *Moments of Truth,*[6] by and about Jan Carlzon, or *Control Your Destiny or Someone Else Will,*[7] by Tichy and Sherman, about (Neutron) Jack Welch, to name a couple. Still interested in good old-fashioned management—you know, the art of getting things done? There's always the Tom Peters' collection, starting with *In Search of Excellence* and his newspaper column "On Excellence"; *Teaching the Elephant to Dance*[8] by James Belasco; or the *One Minute Manager*[9] series, by Blanchard and Johnson.

> Myth associates leadership with superior position. It assumes that when you are on top you are automatically a leader. But leadership is not a place, it is a process. It involves skills and abilities that are useful whether one is in the executive suite or on the front line.[10]

Although *leadership* is not as heinous a word as *management* to most lawyers, it is not embraced either. Most lawyers do not see themselves as people who need to be "led," and they certainly don't have the time to "lead" others. So what could we be thinking in devoting an entire chapter to leadership?

If you accept the precept, cited earlier, that "change has no constituency"[11] you will understand immediately and fully the role of leadership in a changing organization.

> Leadership begins where management ends, where the systems of rewards and punishments, control and scrutiny, give way to innovation, individual character, and the courage of convictions.[12]

We will venture to say that the most important element of a total quality program is its leadership. It will succeed or fail not on the brilliance of its programs or the logic of its processes. It will succeed or fail as a direct consequence of how well it is led.

What exactly does leadership imply and what does it bring to a total quality program that is so essential to the program's success? Vision and long-term goals. Unwavering commitment. Innovation. Communication. Empowerment.

Selecting a Leadership Paradigm

Your selection of a leadership model or paradigm will be very personal. In our organization, we drew individually and as a group from several different sources, including Situational Leadership, developed by Ken Blanchard and Paul Hersey; Stephen Covey's Principle Centered Leadership; and Warren Bennis and his thoughtful writings and discussions on leadership. We learned, as in our application of TQM principles, to look for what made sense to us and our organization. We read and studied the available literature; we drew on those ideas; we personalized them to our individual organization; we incorporated the ideas into our training, management, and quality goals; and then we began the cycle again.

Leadership is not magic. It is a mix of skill and commitment that requires constant practice and sharpening. Continuous improvement applies not only to procedures and products, it also applies to leadership.

Vision and Commitment—You can be assured that very few people in your organization will understand why you are turning everything upside down in this move toward that elusive "total quality thing," and any real benefits will not be clear for one or two years at a minimum. To most people, your total quality program will mean that you're making them spend too much time in meetings or classes; you're disrupting their work life and making simple things—like client service—too complicated. If you react to the moment—to the skepticism and criticism and to the lack of acceptance and understanding—you will end your efforts shortly after you begin. You must see the future and how all the different efforts you are embarking on will come together and transform your organization. This is the most important reason why you cannot simply drop the most current TQM idea into your organization. It must fit into your vision, not the other way around. The same is true of leadership.

As Stephen Covey says, "Begin with the end in mind."[13] What kind of organization do you want to be—or need to be—two, five, or ten years from now? What are your organization's weaknesses? What are its strengths? Spend the time and energy to thoroughly understand what you are trying to accomplish and why it is necessary. Understand how the changes will affect everyone in your organization. If you don't see the future, if you don't understand and believe in the necessity of every step you are taking, you will not be able to withstand the limitless questions and criticisms. You can empathize with those reeling from the changes, but your advocacy of your vision must be relentless.

Take solace, however. As your programs develop and glimpses of the promised future become evident, your vision will be trusted and you will gain commitment to your goals.

Innovation—There's no way around it, innovation and creativity carry risk. If you are willing to try something new, you will take the chance of making a mistake. Notice that we did not say *failure*. Your program will not fail if an innovative approach or program or idea does not work out. You'll simply have to try it a different way. How you move toward your goal is very different from the goal itself. Don't doubt the value or worth of your vision just because you don't hit the mark the first time. You will find better ways of hitting it. You should always be scanning the literature and talking with others about better ways to achieve your total quality goals.

Don't constrain yourself by "the way it's always been." Break the rules; challenge tradition and egos; push to the outer edges. The concept of TQM in a law firm is, in itself, revolutionary. No one knows what to expect next. Take advantage of that to get rid of the "hangnails"—things that everyone possesses, but no one knows why, and that certainly aren't doing anyone any good. You are teaching new rules and setting new standards. If you present them in an innovative, creative way, that very process will say as much as the content itself. Do the unexpected. Draw on ideas and resources outside the legal community. But, as we have stated several times, never simply drop someone else's ideas into your program. You must make them your own.

Communication—Vision is not enough to transform an organization. Unless that vision is clearly communicated, you cannot gain consensus or commitment to your goals. When we think of communicating, we usually think of the written word or the spoken word. Certainly these are two very useful tools. However, the most important form of communication is action.

> Credibility of action is the single most significant determinant of whether a leader will be followed over time.[14]

Your commitment to the goals of your program must be evident in what you say, how you say it, how often you say it, and most important, what you *do*. There can be no exceptions for your friends or your detractors. There can be no running scared. Compromise, if you must, on form, but never on substance.

Empowerment—You cannot do it alone. The climate created by the leader will inspire others to contribute their best. Let others share your vision and collaborate on how to achieve it. Empower the loyalists to be your change agents. They will be on the front line: running the programs, teaching the skills, supporting the goals, and redefining client service. To accomplish great change, you must share the power to make it happen.

Leadership at All Levels

TQM is not simply a top-down or a bottom-up process. It involves everyone in every possible combination, and its leadership cannot be a solo or elitist activity. Although we have gone so far as to invest in leadership training for everyone in our organization, the roles and impact of self-leadership—leading an attorney/secretary office, leading a practice group, and leading the firm—are significantly different. Each leadership level builds on the strengths of the next, until the entire organization is moving forward with shared goals, visions, and commitment. You'll notice that we said "build on the strengths of the next." This is critical. If the highest level of leadership in the organization is weak and ineffectual, it will dilute the potential strength of all other levels.

In your organization you may be faced with a group of outstanding lawyers whose leadership (management) skills are underdeveloped. We suspect also that there has never been a recognized management program in your organization. Depending on where your firm is in its political life cycle or its management and governance maturation cycle, you may still be a dictatorship, an oligarchy, or a democracy, or some combination. Nevertheless, we suggest you need a common language and focus and the ability to "all sing out of the same hymnal" when it comes to leadership and leadership principles.

We reviewed a number of leadership and development programs and decided to embrace the Blanchard Leadership Program. We began with a two-day retreat, led by a facilitator, in which the sole subject was Blanchard's Situational Leadership Program. There was the usual cadre of dissenters and skeptics who were being "held prisoner" at our off-site location; but in the end, we were all more enlightened, and we shared a common vocabulary and experience. Within days, leadership terms easily began to develop in formal and informal discussions. We knew the program had become part of our culture when our section leaders asked for a refresher course. The rest of the firm's lawyers were introduced to the *One Minute Manager*[15] concepts to help them lead their teams, even if those teams consisted of just two people (lawyer and secretary). Our coordinating secretaries (they act as quasi supervisors and help with work flow, etc.) were given a different type of leadership training, which consisted of interpersonal skills development, self-awareness, and problem-solving techniques.

Mentorship

Part and parcel of the whole leadership training approach, and an assurance that the standards and principles we were developing and teaching would be used, was a formalized mentorship program. It became a prime focus for Excellence in Action.

A walk through the history of the firm would provide many excellent examples of mentorship. We found, however, that without a formal program that was carried off with training, feedback, and measurement of results, some associates were "falling through the cracks."

We instituted a structured, formal mentor program that teamed associates with senior partners (shareholders). Mentors were selected for their ability to teach, advise, act as friend and confidant, and problem solve. Mentors also needed to be willing to make a commitment to the program. They needed to be possessed of great patience and listening skills and be able to form a bond of trust and support. They needed to be good communicators. We used the publication *Mentoring, a Practical Guide* by Gordon F. Shea.[16] It is an excellent self-development tool.

Our favorite quote, which says it all:

Mentoring involves going above and beyond. It is a relationship in which a person with greater experience, expertise and wisdom counsels, teaches, guides and helps another person to develop both personally and professionally.

We provided each mentor with Shea's book, held a training session, and then surveyed for results. We concluded early on that for our mentors to be truly effective leaders and resources, some measure of anonymity of the relationship should be recognized. The CEO and a handful of others knew who was paired with whom, but unless the mentee gave specific permission, the mentor was instructed not to give input to the salary and bonus committee or the shareholder evaluation committee (the body that selects new partners).

Leadership and mentoring, therefore, are key to a successful total quality plan. There will be times when these skills will be all you have to take your organization to the next step. Like the song says: "And when I lose my will, you'll be there to push me up the hill."

Making It All Happen

1. Read up on leadership and select from one of the many leadership programs available.

2. Hold a miniretreat off site (two days at most is all you will need) to teach leadership skills. If you do it on site and during work hours there will be too many distractions. Remember, your audience places the same emphasis on things that you do.

3. Follow up on training, and reinforce it by using the vocabulary of the program in discussion and communication.

4. You will need a refresher course within six months. This can be done in less time and on site (assuming there was enough buy-in the first time around).

5. Establish a formalized mentorship program. Select your mentors carefully. Train them. Generally, they should not be people who have formalized supervisory responsibility over the associate.

6. Follow up on the mentorship program through surveys. About six months after the initial training, meet again to improve the process.

Chapter 8

The Role of Training

Stevie Wonder understood: teachin', learnin' will take you not only to higher ground but to the goal of "highest ground." Our training department's mission statement embodied Wonder's words. It said simply: "Our mission is to provide everyone the opportunity to learn and develop the skills and knowledge to contribute their best. . . . "

Building Your Training Department

Bold. Creative. Innovative. Unexpected. Are we sure that we're talking about training here . . . the bastion of forms, procedures, and keystrokes in most law firms? Absolutely. And the quicker you forget what training used to be, you can make it what it should be, the vanguard of your revolution. Design your training department and its role in a way that makes sense to you and your organization. There are no rule books. Once you know what you want to achieve, build your structure around your goals and mission, not the other way around.

Our training department is novel in many ways. As mentioned previously, our firm has placed a tremendous emphasis on how technology can be used in reaching our goal of total quality. We have, therefore, closely aligned our training department with our information systems (computers). We have found that this relationship benefits us continuously. Our course materials and presentation techniques are as high tech as our resources and skills can provide. We also closely integrate the benefits technology can provide in improving quality, efficiency, and client service into our other training goals. Our trainers and application developers work side by side in determining what new technological tools we should develop or introduce, whether they are "easy to use," and how they should be incorporated to achieve our training goals. We also combine the two departments to staff our "help-line" resource for our employees. As a result of this strong relationship, our training has become more holistic in its approach, combining technical and nontechnical elements.

We built our training department from the ground up; we promoted from within, and it is a small department. This forces us to be very open to drawing on whatever other means are available. At times we

People, keep on learn-in!

Teachers, keep on teach-in!

World keep on turn-in

'cause it won't be too long...

till I reach the Highest Ground.

"Higher Ground"
—Stevie Wonder

team-teach classes with senior lawyers, managers, or other specialists and supplement our training with key videotapes. Occasionally we draw on outside resources when necessary and have a reserve of self-teaching tools.

We are disciplined and rigorous in our preparation of course materials. We cannot afford to waste time reconstructing a course. Every training course must have its specific goals identified, a course curriculum, course handouts, and anticipated class schedule prepared with enough time for the drafts to be distributed throughout the department and to others. These drafts are subject to constructive criticism; in fact, we have a policy in our training department that every circulated draft must receive at least one suggested improvement before it is approved. We believe our collective ideas are far better that any of us can produce alone.

We are not above using gimmicks, gifts, or other sundry items to achieve our training goals. Often the best way to get our point across is with the unexpected. We have been known to use play money, Nerf balls, chocolate coins, and other assorted items along with our more traditional course material to emphasize key issues.

We continuously monitor and measure our training's impact. We do this in both traditional and nontraditional ways. In the more traditional vein, written evaluations are completed by participants after every training class, whether it is a classroom or an individual session. We use these evaluations to help us determine how we can improve our training techniques and to ask whether people are using the skills we taught them in their day-to-day jobs.

We also use technology to help us monitor and measure our results. We record all the training goals and requirements of all of our employees in a training database and then record their attendance on a session-by-session basis, along with relevant notes on each attendee and his or her need for follow-up. We use reports from this system to issue periodic transcripts and report cards to our employees and also to quantitatively analyze our success. Our human resources department also uses reports from this system during performance appraisals.

We also employ the technique of peer review to help us measure and monitor in our quarterly "office swap." Remember that once every quarter, secretaries are placed in a different office for a day. At the end of the day, each completes a questionnaire on whether certain "standards" are being followed, and also makes suggestions on areas of improvement. The other benefits of this process are to help develop teamwork skills and to develop a shared personal responsibility and appreciation for firmwide quality.

Balance the old and the new in your training energies. Refer to the volumes of traditional training and development materials, but be selective in your use of them. They will give you ideas, standards, and frameworks, but you must then use your own knowledge of your organization and your creativity to determine what will work best. Be bold, creative, innovative, and have fun.

Moving Toward Total Quality

Once you have committed to continuous total quality, the role of training in transforming your organization is pivotal. It is not enough to say that "things must change." You must provide the organization with a detailed blueprint, and that is done through training.

Much of the initial drive of our Excellence in Action plan came from its training arm. It was through training that we could specifically identify the behavior and attitudes that needed to change or improve. Additionally, a well-designed training program provides an excellent structure to reach everyone in the organization with the same, consistent message said in many different ways.

Many total quality training plans focus primarily on attitudes: If participants understand what "quality" is, they will produce it. Our approach to total quality and training is more pragmatic. We focus on behaviors, establishing clear links between what you do, how you do it, and the importance of its outcome.

To change an organization, you must teach the "new" ways at all levels. If you limit your training program to certain audiences, such as only support staff, you will immediately send a clear message to everyone that quality is a "clerical problem." Your support staff will resent the insinuation, your lofty goals will go unseen and unmet by the lawyers and managers, and the result will be only a few relatively minor changes that are accepted because they were mandated.

To assume that the mere teaching of a new skill, standard, or insight is enough to change a behavior or culture is wishful thinking. You must then monitor and measure whether the new ways have become adopted by your audience. The demand for change may be abrupt, but real change in the behavior and attitude of each individual employee is gradual at best. Don't be dismayed by a lack of overwhelming, immediate change. Allow time for each significant change you teach to become part of your new culture; reinforce the change with monitoring, measuring, and rewarding; teach it again; and then take it a step farther. Design your different training courses to share common themes among them, each reinforcing the others. Additionally, we found that the teaching of complex skills such as technology, leadership, and teamwork is best done in small incremental steps, each step building on the prior one.

Excellence in Action Training Program

Our EIA training program has several different tracks to it, each directly tied to the goals of our EIA plan: Standards and Guidelines, Using Technology, Management and Leadership Skills, Team Building, and Client Service. Each track is offered through parallel programs to the different audiences of support staff, managers, and lawyers. Some of the tracks, such as Standards and Guidelines and Client Service, occur simultaneously to all audiences. Other tracks, such as Using Technology and

Management and Leadership Skills, are carefully timed to introduce new concepts and skills in a certain sequence. Additionally, we offer a series of special supplementary skill-building seminars that focus on the specific needs of a particular audience, such as our paralegals and new associates.

Standards and Guidelines—You must begin at ground zero. This is a significant tenet of our training program. Do not assume without concrete evidence that there is a shared set of common skills, procedures, behaviors, or attitudes among your employees. If you have not built a solid foundation of basic skills, you risk wasting a tremendous amount of time, energy, and resources. You will confuse your audiences and lose one of your most important strengths—credibility. If your employees lose faith in the ability of the training department to identify and correct areas of weakness in the organization and in individuals, you will be severely handicapped in your future attempts to teach anything new.

You can assess your starting point in several ways: formal assessment tests, prior training history, observation, problem referrals, questionnaires, and forums or roundtables.

We used the formal assessment technique to determine the level of technological skills our employees had mastered. This "testing" approach works best when you can easily measure the ability of someone to perform specific tasks, such as identifying the correct keystrokes in a word-processing program. We will discuss our technology assessment test in more detail in the following section, "Using Technology." We also drew some conclusions about office and file management techniques through observation and referrals to the training department for problem resolution. We conducted a thorough review of the attendees at our prior training courses and our notes at that time. Although we had an inkling of the disparity in knowledge of even the most "basic" skills and procedures, we verified this with asking key questions both in written questionnaires and in forums targeted to the different audiences.

From all of this evidence, we determined that our first step toward providing quality service for our clients was to ensure a strong shared base of essential skills. Our first year of training was devoted to the basic skills required by each audience.

Several sessions of each class were scheduled over one or two months in order to accommodate everyone. The classes generally lasted from a few hours to a half day. Following is a list of our core EIA classes:

Schedule of EIA Classes for Secretaries

Organizing your Office	Professionalism and Ethics
Time Management	Client Service
Open/Closing Files	Billing Guidelines
Getting Assistance	Managing Your Files
Preparation of Pleadings	Stress Management

Schedule of EIA Classes for Administrative Staff

Organizing Your Work Space	Professionalism and Ethics
Phone and	Time Management
Communication Skills	Client Service
Internal Client Service	Grammar and Writing Skills
Handling Difficult People	Stress Management

Schedule of EIA Classes for Paralegals

Defining Your Role	Professionalism and Ethics
Managing Your Office	Time Management
Billing Guidelines	Client Service
Managing Your Files	Preparation of Pleadings
Stress Management	

Schedule of EIA Classes for Attorneys

Managing Your Office	Professionalism and Ethics
Time Management	Client Service
Open/Closing Files	Billing Guidelines
Getting Assistance	Managing Your Files
Preparation of Pleadings	Stress Management

Pay particular attention to the way that the secretary and lawyer programs parallel each other. Change cannot occur unless the entire team is moving in the same direction. Additionally, you can see that there are common themes present in all of the tracks.

After we determined the schedule of class topics, we went back to our employees to help us determine topic content. We asked our employees for their ideas and suggestions on what should be standardized. We asked them to offer us their "best" practices. We had a series of several open meetings with our support staff on each topic. We distributed and received written questionnaires completed by lawyers and support staff alike. We drew from the input of our employees to develop our "standards" and course curriculum. An additional benefit proved to be consensus on the need for standardization in the firm.

We were very careful in our use of the word *standard*. A "standard" had to meet the following test: It was required to achieve a quality goal, and it could be practiced universally by everyone. We supplemented our use of "standards" with "recommended practices." These recommendations were not required, but were offered as the most efficient or "best" way.

The quality of course material and presentation affects the credibility an audience assigns it. We prepared all of our course material on desktop publishing. We ordered special binders to hold the course materials. When we discussed the value of organizing and prioritizing, for example, we provided our students with EIA folders and to-do lists. When we introduced the concept of managing to our lawyers, managers, and paralegals, we provided each of them with a copy of *One Minute Manager*[1] prior to class for their study. We occasionally supplemented our course material with carefully selected videotapes.

Similar care should be taken in determining who should teach the courses. Draw on all available resources in making your selection. Our secretarial and administrative classes were generally taught by members of our training department. Many of our lawyer and paralegal classes, however, were team taught with lawyers of significant stature in the firm.

Pay attention to when you should keep your audiences separate and when you should combine them in training sessions. For example, there was a distinct difference in our training focus in the secretarial Organizing Your Office class, with its emphasis on procedural and organizational techniques and standards, and the lawyers' Managing Your Office class, with its introduction of "management/leadership" responsibilities. On the other hand, the major procedural changes taught in our Billing Guidelines class required that entire teams (lawyer, paralegal, secretary) attend them together.

Attendance at these core classes was mandatory. Failure to attend was met with forceful reminders. This is critical. Your message must be heard by everyone without excuse. Your employees will place the same amount of value on your training program that your organization and its leaders do.

Using Technology—We believe that it is only with the skilled use of the technological tools we provide our employees that our goals of improved efficiency, quality, and client service can be achieved. Easier said than done, especially when the most frequent comment we heard from our lawyers went something like this: "You mean I have to use that thing?"

Our challenge was twofold: First, we had to make sure that our applications and software made sense to our users and our goals; second, we had to ensure that our employees could skillfully use them. We will discuss our use of technology in more detail in Chapter 9, "The Role of Technology."

First, determine what technology encompasses. In our firm it means not only the computer system and its many resident software applications including LEXIS and Westlaw, but also telephones, voice mail, facsimile, photocopy cost recovery, dictating machines, copy machines, and so forth. We also felt that providing training and support for home personal computer use and connection to our central computer system was a service the training department should provide our employees.

Your next step is to determine what people need to know. This will differ among and within each audience. Start with the current job descriptions, and then envision how the use of technology would enhance their efficiency and quality of work. Understand thoroughly the future goals of your organization and how technology can be used to reach them. For example, we see the implementation of firmwide knowledge banks containing information such as client guidelines, work product, case and docket information, and expert witness material as an essential part of our total quality plan.

Itemize specifically how each technological tool, current and planned, should be used by each type of employee; what tools are critical to do their immediate job; what tools are critical to your organization's accomplishing its goals (there may be a difference); what training is needed immediately and what can wait.

Now that you've determined what your employees need to know, find out what they do know, what they don't know, and what they're doing wrong. We used a "Skills Assessment" tool to accomplish this. This assessment was tailored to the expected job skills of each category of employee, including novice secretary, senior secretary, supervising secretary, associate lawyer, senior partner, and administrative clerical staff. Every employee underwent an appraisal that asked them to use different technological tools to perform specified tasks. If they were unable to use the tool accurately, then they were "registered" to attend an upcoming training class on that topic.

Our technological training was done both in classroom sessions of up to six participants and on an individual basis. The individual sessions were most popular with our lawyers and were often held ad hoc as a result of a Help-Line call. It is essential that technological training be structured incrementally, especially with novices. Too much, too soon is a common problem, especially with computer training of lawyers. Technological training must be very structured, and sequential in its presentation and supporting materials. Class handouts should be designed to be used as a self-teaching refresher course. Make them of the highest quality in terms of clarity and consistency.

We made sure that there were close ties between our Standards classes and our technological training. For example, it was a standard that employees use our automated case management and calendaring system on a regular basis to update and keep a record of their files. We coordinated classes in technology to either teach anew or refresh our employees' skills in using this application. Another example is related to our File Opening class, where we taught the standard of referring to our automated client guidelines system for information on how clients prefer their files to be handled. Our client guidelines system is an electronic catalog of the instructions and preferences of our clients, including topics such as billing, reporting, methods of communication, alternative dispute resolution, and final disposition.

We use our help-line as a continuing training tool, using every opportunity to teach new skills, offer a "better" way, or correct "bad habits." We place a strong emphasis on making the most of these one-on-one situations to strengthen our employees' technological skills. We strive to be an ongoing resource for our employees, immediately responsive to their requests for assistance or training.

Management and Leadership Skills—A basic premise of our EIA training program is that developing leadership skills is beneficial to everyone in our firm, regardless of position. Leadership is not seen as an elite activity, demonstrated by only a few members of the upper management (president/CEO, board of directors, section leaders). It is expected from everyone but may be demonstrated in different ways, depending on their role in the organization: self-leadership; acting as a coordinating secretary; leading a lawyer/secretary office; mentoring; leading a practice section; representing the firm on the board of directors; and leading the firm as president/CEO.

We wanted to develop a leadership training program that could help develop skills at all levels. We reviewed a number of leadership programs to find one that met that criterion. We selected the Situational Leadership paradigm. This model was first developed by Ken Blanchard and Paul Hersey. It was then developed further by Ken Blanchard, and his version was named Situational Leadership II. Our understanding and implementation of this model drew on Paul Hersey's *The Situational Leader*[2] and from extensive material developed by Blanchard Training and Development for Situational Leadership II.

Very simply put, Situational Leadership involves developing the leadership skills to adjust your style (the amount of direction and/or emotional support you provide) to your follower's level of commitment and readiness (ability to perform the specific task). It is based on the important premise that the amount of direction and/or emotional support required may vary, depending on the specific situation or task you ask someone to perform. It is a developmental model, based on the belief that as people's skill and commitment increase, their need for direction and emotional support decreases.

Leadership training began for the senior leaders of our firm with a two-day off-site retreat. Attending this retreat were the president/CEO, board of directors, and section leaders. The retreat focused on introducing the concepts of Situational Leadership II. It was led by a senior facilitator from the Blanchard group. Although there was, as expected, some initial resistance to spending so much time discussing nonlegal issues, by the end of the retreat a common language and understanding had been established.

We used the book *One Minute Manager* by Ken Blanchard, to introduce some basic concepts of leadership to our lawyers and coordinating secretaries. This book discusses leadership as it applies to the use of goal setting, recognition, and reprimand in developing employees' potential. The next step in leadership training was to merge the *One Minute Manager* and Situational Leadership II concepts. We used the *Leadership and the One Minute Manager*[3] book and videotape by the Blanchard group to help us accomplish this.

Another aspect of the Situational Leadership II model is how it can be used as a self-leadership tool. Blanchard Training and Development has used this approach in its Situational Self-Leadership material. The purpose of the approach is to help individual employees learn how to assess their level of readiness and commitment for a given task and to learn to better identify and ask for the amount and type of direction and support they need from their leader.

Team Building—At the very start of our total quality program, we performed some serious self-analysis of our organization to identify its strengths and weaknesses. An obvious and apparent weakness was in the area of teamwork, yet we knew that the goals of total quality demanded an increased ability to work together and achieve common goals. Building teamwork was an essential requirement to reach our total quality goals.

We used the Teamworking/Building High Performing Teams material developed by Blanchard Training and Development in our team-building sessions. This material uses the Situational Leadership model and applies it to the developmental stages that groups go through to become effective teams. Without effective leadership, however, groups can get "stuck" in an early stage. Effectively moving the group through the different stages depends on the leadership ability of the group leader.

This team-building program also helps individual members of a group identify how they can help a team work better together. They assess what they bring to the group as individuals: how their talents, personality strengths and weaknesses, and conflict resolution styles affect the team's performance.

In summary, the role of training in total quality is that of providing the vehicle to take you to the "Highest Ground." Give training your total support.

Making It All Happen

1. You must commit time, money, and effort to training. It is a large component of your total quality plan and of what you will do.

2. If you do not have a training department, you can build one from the ground up. We did it by posting the positions for application with job descriptions and minimum qualifications. We should not have been, but we were, amazed at the wealth of talent in the training area that we found right in our own firm. We promoted from within.

3. Give your trainers the freedom, the tools (technical or otherwise), and the authority to carry out their mission.

4. The plan and direction of training was a constant subject of discussion between the training department and senior management, but the method and means were most often left to their collective creative genius. Pick the right people and let them do the job.

5. Use teachers from outside the firm if need be, but make sure they can make their subject matter relevant to the law business.

6. Training has to be universal to meet the "total" aspect of total quality. Training was therefore mandatory. It was monitored and measured.

7. Have your trainees evaluate both the program and the teachers. We did not have the luxury of time to reconstruct a course, but we were flexible enough to make changes when necessary.

8. Follow up with measurement of the application of the training and its effectiveness with questionnaires, assessments, "the office swap" (where a secretary spends the day in another office), and reminders. For instance, after the Time Management class for lawyers, the section leaders followed up in their meetings by asking each lawyer to relate how one thing he or she learned was incorporated into the practice.

Chapter 9

The Role of Technology

In 1987, we purchased our third generation of computer technology. It consisted of the most powerful tools available at the time, so we named the system "Superman." Today, we might more appropriately have called it "Ben." Masters of the art of computer technology will relate to the lyrics above, since most lawyers over the age of thirty have an immediate and visceral negative reaction to the legal computer tool, which is much the same reaction that moviegoers initially had when a little boy befriended a rat in the movie *Ben*. Our trainers and technical people knew that the lawyers did not see the computer as they did, but wished sincerely that they would try. For if they did, they would see they had a friend in "Ben."

We have built many of the elements of our Excellence in Action program on the unlikely marriage of technology and total quality. We consider technology to include computers, phones, voice mail, telecommunication, facsimile, and scanning devices, but our primary emphasis in this chapter is on our use of computers. Our approach has demanded that we build consensus on the use of technology that goes beyond the basics. Most lawyers, after they get over their initial negative reaction, will still see computers as an evil, albeit a necessary one. Grudgingly, there is the acceptance that it is perhaps foolish, if not impossible, to do business in today's environment without a level of technological finesse—word processing, phones, facsimile, time and billing, electronic legal research. But taking it beyond these basics—that's another story. Resistance is too weak a word to describe the general reaction of most lawyers to what they consider "unnecessary" technology.

To keep costs down for clients, we embarked on a program of asking fewer people to do more. But how do you reconcile this goal with an ever-increasing client demand for continuous improvement in quality, productivity, and efficiency? Use technology as your workhorse. Harness the power of technology and use it to provide easier, faster, and better ways of doing routine tasks. Use it as a central warehouse of knowledge and experience easily shared and accessed by everyone. Use it as a communications tool between your organization and your clients.

They don't see you as I do;
I wish they would try to;
I'm sure they'd think again
if they had a friend like
Ben.

"Ben"
—The Jackson Five

Technology as a Client Service

The cost of technology makes it hard to ignore, and many law firms have sought ways to recoup some of that investment. This usually translates into charging clients for many uses of technology. It is therefore tempting to judge litigation support or other computer-assisted, case-specific activities on their ability to generate profits. Investment in the development of "firm" applications, such as case management, unfortunately often is scrutinized in terms of its ability to provide immediate payback.

Our use of technology challenged this conventional approach. We determined early on that technology should be used to enhance client service without any additional charge to the client. We believed that the resulting differentiation and competitive edge we gained with our clients far outweighed our costs. As a result, much of our information management strategy was focused on application development that enhanced our internal productivity and efficiency and improved communications with our clients while insuring a high-quality work product. In addition to the basic off-the-shelf applications of word processing, time and billing, and electronic legal research, we designed and developed the following custom applications: case management and calendaring, practice development, expert witness, human resource management, attorney profile and expertise, client guidelines, work product bank, litigation support, and a transcript pool. All of these applications were closely tied to our total quality efforts. If you are part of a smaller organization, do not automatically assume these tools are too expensive to develop. The price and performance curves come together quickly.

Developing an Information Management Strategy

Many law firms are beginning to see the value of strategic planning when focusing on niche markets or new client development. However, the issues related to information management and the use of computers and technology are rarely considered strategic concerns in law firms. This is a critical oversight. As Roger K. Sullivan, BIS Strategic Decisions, stated:

> Rapid business change is a given for the '90s. Information will become more complex and impossible to manage with conventional systems. Technology and process innovation are survival necessities. Effective information management is a competitive necessity.[1]

Or, closer to home, consider the following:

> Must litigators use computers or face malpractice? At what point does technological development cease being personal preference or business efficiency? When does technology become a professional and legal imperative? Should lawyers be obligated to employ technology that results in better service to their clients?[2]

As a result of these questions and concerns, we spent time on a continuing basis to ensure that our use of technology was consistent with our firm goals and our client needs.

A few years ago we analyzed our use of technology and found that it centered primarily on information processing, i.e., using specific computer tools to perform tasks. The major emphasis was on processing data in applications such as word processing, time and billing, and some database applications. The focus was on production—getting the work out.

We determined that our firm goals of continuous total quality and improved efficiency and productivity required a change in focus. An evolution from information *processing* to information *management* was essential. Information management focuses on providing easy access to the expansive collection of "firm information." We identified the firm's collective knowledge and experience as our *knowledgebase*. It was one of the cornerstones of our strategy and resulted in greater emphasis on lawyer tools and decision support systems. We also determined that technology should be used to publish, monitor, and support standards of excellence.

Common Shared Knowledgebase

As stated above, one of the foundations of our information management strategy is that there is easy access to the firm's knowledgebase. This strategy has resulted in several concrete actions and developments.

Similar to many other large firms, we have several branch offices. Many of our offices share the same client base. For a time, these offices acted as separate islands of information. Sharing information was tedious at best. Access to information stored on our central main computer system was possible, but access to information stored at other branch offices was impossible without the intervention of the systems department. Even when access to the central system was possible, extra steps were necessary —a choice could be made to access such information or not. This is significantly different from structuring a system where access to the firm's shared information is the way you do your job. No choice allowed. Thus, our strategy changed. We required that everyone easily and instantaneously access the firm knowledgebase. All of our offices became linked via telecommunications and accessed a shared shared computer system, but more importantly, its knowledgebase. Our clients benefited from the firm's collective experience and knowledge, regardless of where their matter was being handled geographically.

In the same vein, we developed guidelines for the handling of personal information and firm information. Personal information is data that are individual and private to the employee. Such data does not need to be accessed or shared by anyone else. We provided a list of supported software to handle this personal information, provided training and recommendations on the use of the software, but we do not monitor it in any other way. Lawyers and staff can store any information they desire.

Firm information, on the other hand, constitutes the majority of information handled by our computer systems. It includes all the data that may need to be accessed at any time by another lawyer, support staff, or client. This information requires standard guidelines for its use, storage, and retrieval. It is this use and storage of firm information that is closely aligned with our total quality program.

The Marriage of Technology and Total Quality

Many of our quality standards and goals are closely linked to our use of technology. Several of our custom applications come to mind immediately: case management system, expert witness system, client guidelines, and work product retrieval, to name a few.

Our case management system serves as a central storage for case and calendaring information about every matter handled by our firm. A variety of case-specific information is stored in each case record, including such basic information as the identity of all the players, financial data, narratives of upcoming plans and significant events, and final disposition information. Additionally, every significant calendar, docket, and diary date is stored in calendar entries for each case.

As we see it, the benefits of this application increase the farther you get from the individual handling lawyer's office. If you are the responsible lawyer (as distinct from the handling or billing lawyer) and receive a call from the client, you can have an immediate update of the case and its status within a few seconds. Additionally, if you are a practice section leader and are responsible for overseeing the handling of all matters in your section, you have all the necessary information in a few keystrokes. Most significantly, if you are the client and want an immediate update on the status of your case, what has occurred and what is planned, you can have this information electronically at your convenience. In addition, many of our quality guidelines require specifics such as periodic journalizing of cases for evaluation and routine case status reports to clients. These kinds of activities are easily and consistently generated through our case management system.

In the litigation practice, we are in the age of the expert. Being able to find information quickly about proposed experts or suggestions on available recommended experts is key. We have stored information about the thousands of experts our firm has used or been exposed to over the years in one central system called the expert witness system.

In addition to information about each expert, including his or her specific expertise, we also store detailed information about the many thousands of documents we possess related to all experts. These include deposition and trial transcripts, curricula vitae, and other reports. Our ability to access this information quickly saves unnecessary time and expense and provides our clients with the best of our collective experience and knowledge instantaneously.

Our client guidelines system is probably the clearest example of technology's being directly linked with enhancing client service. This system stores all the guidelines, preferences, procedures, and requirements that our clients provide us in the handling of a matter. In the past, our manual system tried to ensure that the correct copies of the many memos and letters relating to client requests were sent to the appropriate lawyers handling the matters. In reality, however, there was no systematic way to determine clients' preferences in the handling of their matters. This information is now stored electronically.

When a file is opened and received by the handling lawyer, there is only one place where that lawyer has to look for the current, up-to-date client guideline on billing format and cycle, reporting requirements, expert handling, discovery and trial management, alternative dispute resolution, and so forth. In addition, this system stores those other preferences that are often communicated via telephone calls to senior lawyers, or issued by the responsible senior lawyers themselves. Doing things the way the client wants—client service—is now much easier to ensure. If clients do not present a protocol, we inquire. After learning of their preferences, we create a protocol for them.

The product of law firms is represented by the research, pleadings, and other documents prepared in the handling of matters. These "work products" are at the core of a law firm's expertise, knowledge, and experience. What if it were possible for everyone in the law firm to benefit from the best of that knowledge and experience? That was the central concept of our work product retrieval bank. This application stores the "best" motions and briefs, research memoranda, opinion letters, contracts, voir dire questions, and many other work-product documents. Lawyers are able to access this system and search for documents using a variety of criteria, cataloged by type and topic. They can then use these documents as a base for their product or select standard formats that have been previously prepared. Many clients refuse to pay for routine research and preparation of pleadings. They feel that they are paying for the knowledge and experience of the firm, and should not have to repeatedly pay for "reinventing the wheel." We agree. The system makes it all happen.

Other Uses of Technology

In addition to the applications described above, we use technology to help us monitor and measure quality results. For example, we contact our clients at the close of every file and have them rate us on key quality indicators. We call this our *End-of-Matter Report Card*. We store these responses as quantitative values in a database, and we are able to analyze and measure problem areas and trends of improvement. As described in our chapter on training, we use our training database to store the results of our skills assessment and completed classes and training. We also use our practice development system to track contacts made with our existing and potential clients and review on a monthly basis the number of matters received and how that number compares with the prior year.

Litigation support is, most often, the use of computers to assist in the management of complex cases. It involves storing document summaries or indexes online as well as storing the full texts of deposition and trial transcripts. The use of computers in litigation support is often critical when managing voluminous documents or comparing testimony in hundreds of transcripts. We offer this service and our expertise in this area to our clients as a tool to enhance the quality and efficient handling of our clients' cases.

Technology and Training

You can have the most sophisticated computer system in the world, but if it is not being used, it is worthless. Our information management strategy emphasizes that we provide our lawyers and support staff with a flexible, incremental, outstanding training program that is responsive to the different needs of our varied users. We provide technological training in classroom settings, one-on-one, during lunch hours, during off-hours, and with self-paced modules. Training is viewed as ongoing and continuous, with a full menu of offerings always available. Training is task-oriented, and classes are often organized by skill level, practice area, client needs, or application.

As described in Chapter 8, "The Role of Training," we make sure that there are close ties between our "standards" classes and our technology training. All of our "standards" classes have links with our use of technology. When we taught the necessity of routine journalizing and case status review in our Organizing/Managing Your Office class, we required that the dates and data be entered in our case management system. At the same time, special emphasis was placed on providing refresher courses on the use of the case management system, along with detailed instructions on how the data should be entered in the system. Our Client Service and Opening and Closing Files classes discussed the required use of several of our applications in the handling of files: issuance of engagement letters, of which recommended samples are stored in word processing; review of the client guidelines system for instructions on clients' preferences; review of the practice development system to measure whether client satisfaction can be seen through the results of the end-of-matter report cards or through an increase in matters received; the entry of required information in the case management system when a file is first opened and when it is closed. At the time these standards and others were taught in the standards classes, frequent technology classes and one-on-one training on the "how-to's" of using these systems were also offered.

Support is an essential element of the successful use of technology. Help must be immediately available when difficulty arises, and answers must be provided in a language that your users can understand. Our combined Information Systems and Training departments staff the Help Line and provide assistance to our users during regular office hours. The combined departments know not only how to use the applications but also how they are to be used in our continuing quest for total quality.

Positioning for the Future

As part of our information strategy, we developed a thorough mission statement that details how our use of technology, training, and support will help accomplish the firm's goals of total quality and continuous improvement. Here is the final paragraph of our Information Management Mission Statement that speaks to the needs of the future:

> Technology changes. It changes at an extremely rapid pace. We must always have one foot in the here and now and the other in the future. We must thoroughly understand our own needs and requirements and not be seduced by technology for technology's sake alone. We must stay focused and committed to the goals as stated in our and the Firm's Mission Statements.

We have a friend in Ben.

Making It All Happen

1. Make the transition from information processing to information management. You probably have made the investment in the hardware; now it's time to invest in the people necessary to make the hardware and software do all it can do for you.

2. Integrate what you are doing; make your firm's base of knowledge universally available.

3. Develop customized software that is user-specific for your organization. Here are some that might be givens:

   • Case Management and Calendaring System

   • Litigation Support System, including an Expert Witness System if you have a significant litigation practice

   • Client Guidelines Database

   • Work Product Database

   • Lawyer Profile and Expertise Bank

   • Practice Development System

   • Human Resource Management

4. **Case Management and Calendaring System**. Our CMS is a practice management tool designed to track, summarize, and monitor case information and activity. It provides a central storage point that can be commonly shared among lawyers, support staff and clients. A detailed summary of the case is stored on the case record. In addition, lawyers' calendars and case calendars are a database on this system.

5. **Litigation Support and Expert Witness systems.** The Litigation Support System is used to manage complex cases involving massive amounts of documents or testimony, while the Expert Witness System is a database of experts' names, area of expertise, and a summary of documents on file or available from other sources.

6. **Client Guidelines Database.** Nearly all new clients have a written protocol, guideline, or procedure. If they don't, you should create one for them. What are their reporting requirements? How often do you report and to whom? When will bills be generated and in what format? And so on.

7. **Work Product Retrieval Database.** This is a must. Most clients want to make a commodity out of legal work. It is a laudable (and reasonable, we believe) goal. After all, it will surely reduce

legal costs, i.e., the wheel will not have to be reinvented. We would suggest that legal services are not quite as generic as wheels, but will admit that many tasks can be made commodities.

8. **Lawyer Profile and Expertise Bank.** You will be pleasantly surprised at the legal and nonlegal expertise that exists in your firm that you did not know about. You will find everything from antitrust to zoning, airline pilots to zoologists. It makes for a great marketing tool and pool of information. Do a survey to gather the information. Appendix G is an example.

9. **Practice Development System**. Do you ever get the feeling that your client development budget is not allocated correctly or your client development dollar is not being spent in the way you intended it? Track it; you'll be surprised.

10. **Human Resource Management**. Basic personnel information— the employees' application, references, testing scores, or writing samples, together with performance appraisals—make up this database.

11. Assuming you have invested in the people who can "make the technology happen," give them the power to effect changes in your system to constantly achieve improvement.

Client Service—
The Quest for Quality
Will Never End

We have demonstrated that total quality, the process, can be applied to a law firm, and we have the experience to know that initially it is something like a revolution. The real progress will come from the evolutionary stage, and will only be evidenced over time. Although we were able to change the culture of a large firm, we preserved those things that were important to us, such as the close-knit family feeling that prevailed across the organization. We changed whatever needed to be changed to address the legal services marketplace of the 1990s, including the ability to partner with existing and new clients for our mutual benefit.

But here is the $64,000 question that we're sure you're asking. We have established new processes and procedures; we have changed the way we do business; but has the program really been successful? What has it done for our firm, and more important, what has it done for our clients?

We believe that our total quality program, Excellence in Action, is really just the first step toward continuous improvement and total quality. The final chapter has not been written yet, nor can it be. The management gurus will tell you that the effects of even the most comprehensive plan are not felt immediately; the steps up the improvement stairway are taken one by one, slowly and surely.

But you did not read this book only to hear at the end that we have no conclusions about our program and its worth. You probably read this book with one main question in mind: Did our program work? It is worth investing the time and energy of your firm in a total quality program? What are the benefits and payoffs of such an investment?

Malcolm Baldrige Award Criteria

During the early planning stages of our total quality program, we read about the Malcolm Baldrige Award in the lay press. Although it appeared initially that the criteria for winning the award might not make sense for a law firm, we delved into it deeply to see what guidance it

Reach out and touch somebody's hand,

Make this world a better place if you can.

Take a little time out of your busy day,

To give encouragement to someone who's lost the way.

Or would I be talking to a stone if I asked you to share a problem that's not your own. We can change things if we start giving.

Why don't you Reach Out

And...Touch Somebody's Hand

**"Reach Out and Touch (Somebody's Hand)"
—Diana Ross**

might provide. We found that as we began to adapt the ideas and process-es outlined, it helped us immensely. How to fully adapt the criteria could be the subject of yet another endeavor, but suffice it to say here that it can be useful to implement total quality techniques.

The total quality movement in America began in the manufactur-ing sector primarily as a response to foreign competition. To encourage businesses to invest in quality initiatives, Congress established the Malcolm Baldrige National Quality Award in 1987 as a way to recognize U.S. companies that excel in quality management and quality achieve-ment. The award promotes awareness of quality as an increasingly impor-tant element in competitiveness. In the years since its creation, it has become the established benchmark against which all businesses measure themselves in terms of quality and improved operations. Application for consideration of the Malcolm Baldrige Award requires a business to com-pete on the basis of seven criteria:

1. Leadership
2. Information and Analysis
3. Strategic Quality Planning
4. Human Resource Development and Management
5. Management of Process Quality
6. Quality and Operational Results
7. Customer Focus and Satisfaction

When reviewing an application, the Baldrige examiners look for three factors in each criteria: *Approach,* which refers to the processes you use to achieve quality product services; *Deployment,* which refers to how well your approach has been executed; and *Results.*

Using the stringent criteria of the Malcolm Baldrige Award, how did our EIA program specifically affect our organization and our clients?

Leadership

The Baldrige standard requires that the leaders of a business create a client service orientation and establish clear and visible quality values and high expectations. They must take part in the creation of strategies, systems, and methods of achieving excellence.

Our quality initiative was visibly driven by the firm leadership. Our president and CEO, board of directors, and section leaders were per-sonally and visibly involved in the quality-related activities and programs. They taught the classes and monitored the quality of workproduct and the level of client satisfaction; they were directly involved in examining and restructuring business processes and procedures (reengineering, as it is known in the TQM world); they continuously communicated our quality values and goals in formal and informal sessions. The leaders of our firm supported and participated in employee recognition and mentoring pro-grams as well as focus groups and informal brainstorming sessions.

Using this criterion, the leadership of our quality program had been clear, visible, and directly involved in all of its facets.

Information and Analysis

The Baldrige Award requires that quality and operational management be based on reliable information, data, and analysis. Accurate internal measurement tools as well as comparisons with "best practices" benchmarks are required in determining a company's performance.

EIA was built on, and continually validated against, several types of information and data, both internal and external. The results of our client satisfaction survey, detailed in percentages and graphs, were the force behind much of our initiative. We altered many of our processes (specifically, the manner of opening our files, our approach to billing, and our responsiveness to clients). Although the results of follow-up independent client surveys have not yet been revealed, we at least now have clear benchmarks against which to measure gains in client satisfaction. In a less formal way, we have built the idea of client surveys into our everyday business practice through the end-of-matter report cards. This gives us one tool to measure and detail improving client satisfaction.

We also built internal measurements into every part of our quality program. We utilized several tools, including evaluation of our training classes, recording increases and decreases in employee recognition nominations, distributing and recording responses by our associates every thirty days on the frequency and type of contact they had with their mentors, and tracking client development activities and client satisfaction (end-of-matter report cards). We more accurately identified quality employee behavior through improved performance appraisal forms. We kept records of the number and types of new matters and clients coming into the firm and, of course, kept close tabs on our profitability.

Based on these measurement tools, we established a process beginning with data collected that result in changed procedures, processes, or programs, at which point the process of monitoring and measuring begins again.

We would like to share the results of two significant measurements taken at the start of our quality program and again at the time of this book's publication: First, the number of new matters and clients coming into the firm increased to record levels over previous years; second, the financial profitability of the firm also increased over prior years.

Strategic Quality Planning

The Baldrige criterion maintains that achieving quality and market leadership requires a business to have a strong future orientation and a willingness to make long-term commitments to clients, employees, suppliers, and the community. Long-term planning strategies must determine or anticipate the types of changes that may affect clients' expectations.

Although we are much better at defining long-term goals and measuring our progress, or lack thereof, against business and marketing plans, strategic quality planning is still an area of weakness for us. Much of our planning is carried around in the heads of senior lawyers and administration. Too much time spent in strategic planning sessions is still viewed as overly bureaucratic and unnecessary. There is a belief that strategic planning only complicates the simple process of providing quality legal work. Soon the market pressures will give us no choice. As we pointed out earlier, when it gets to the point that government gets involved in a big way, even the most skeptical among us must pay heed. Witness the passage and signing into law of the Government Performance and Results Act of 1993, which requires U.S. agencies to have strategic plans.

Human Resource Development and Management

This Baldrige criterion focuses on the close link between employee satisfaction and customer satisfaction and, in fact, describes it as a "shared fate" relationship. Employee satisfaction is seen as an important indicator of the company's efforts to improve client satisfaction and operating performance.

As we indicated in Chapter 1, a driving force behind our EIA program was the results of our employee survey. Many of the programs we began through EIA addressed the results of that survey. There was a request for more and better in-house training. As we described in Chapter 8, our training program is now quite extensive and goes beyond the traditional law firm idea of training. We track the individual training goals of all employees and work with them to achieve the skill levels they need to perform their jobs. We use our training program to teach quality standards and more efficient and effective ways of performing tasks.

Our training department also gets involved in needs assessment as our organization experiences change. For example, as the ratio of secretaries to lawyers decreased, the training department surveyed the firm and helped identify how jobs were being changed. What was the impact of those changes on client service, quality, productivity, and efficiency? What were the "best practices" to share with the rest of the firm? And what additional training (e.g., teambuilding, conflict resolution) was required?

Another result of the employee survey was a request for more positive recognition of employees. As described previously, we established several employee recognition programs. We also taught lawyers management skills, including acknowledging and praising good work. We can now state that positive employee recognition has become an established aspect of our firm culture.

We found it difficult, however, to accurately measure an increase or a decrease in employee satisfaction. We found that every time a change was introduced, the general initial reaction was negative, whether or not we were providing a requested service (e.g., improved training). And because our program required so much change in such a short period of time, we found that we could not accurately separate out the general effects of change from other measurements of employee satisfaction. We will, however, continue to measure employee satisfaction through employee surveys and will continue to make necessary changes in our culture and business.

From a quantitative point of view we did see an increase in training, participation in employee recognition programs, focus group participation, mentoring programs, and so forth. We also successfully reduced the ratio of secretaries to lawyers while achieving our goals of improved client service, efficiency, and productivity, and a substantially reduced overtime budget. Our investments in technology and training paid off here. We found that even with high levels of new matters coming into the firm, we were doing more with fewer people.

Management of Process Quality

The Baldrige criterion is based on the premise that quality systems must place a strong emphasis on design quality: that is, problem and waste prevention are achieved through building quality not only into the products and services but also into the actual processes that produce them. Success in competitive markets requires a faster, more flexible response to clients' requirements while offering new or improved services.

At the start of our EIA program, we would never have believed how much progress we would make in the area of "workflow redesign" in such a short period of time. Our success in this area has exceeded our highest expectations. As described in Chapter 6, we thoroughly examined many of our business processes and procedures and made significant and dramatic changes in them. One example includes our changes to our billing system to provide information to clients in the way they want it, and to increase flexibility in how the information is presented and delivered (e.g., electronically) to them. We also discussed in Chapter 6 the changes to the way we open files and our initial handling of them to ensure faster response and better communication to our clients. We modified the way we close files and built in a system to keep continuous close tabs on client satisfaction with the end-of-matter report cards.

Operationally, we reexamined how we were staffed and made some difficult changes to improve our efficiency without any compromise to our goal of improving quality and client service.

We also found ourselves much better able to understand and respond to our clients' requests (e.g., RFPs) to "partner" for "continuous improvement" and "improve the processes" of what we were doing for them. Focus groups brainstormed new approaches to litigation and alternative fee arrangements. We talked about how to manage the process of litigation better. Our EIA program and our own experience in workflow redesign positioned us to respond successfully.

We also continued to look to technology and how we could use it for better design of quality systems. Internally, and with our clients, communication is at a level unlike, we believe, any other firm, and better communication means more efficiency and higher quality service. Using E-mail rather than the hated "inner-office memorandum" allows our lawyers to review a pile of "memos" in a matter of seconds without the use of paper. Simple things like delivery to courts, finding assistance, and searching for an expert or document are communicated to the entire firm instantaneously.

We are definitely looking at things in a new way and are proactively looking at all of our processes to see how they can be improved.

Quality and Operational Results

The Baldrige criterion provides a results focus for all quality system actions. It represents the link between client requirements and the quality system. It is through this focus that the purpose of quality—to provide superior value, as viewed by the client, along with superior company performance as demonstrated in productivity, efficiency, and effectiveness—is maintained.

Let's look at the numbers. The number of new matters coming in from new and existing clients has continuously increased. That is certainly one measure of quality and operational results, as well as confidence in our work product; but are there other measurements? What percentage of a client's book of legal business are we getting? What percentage can we get? We will continue to get better answers to these questions.

We can report that for the duration of our EIA program our profitability has improved, in spite of the time and money spent in its planning, development, and implementation.

We can report an increase in employee participation in training and recognition programs. And we have successfully improved our efficiency in staffing, evidenced by our reduced secretary-to-lawyer ratio.

We are continuing to measure the effects of our improved processes and workflows through the end-of-matter report cards. We expect to see increasing levels of client satisfaction as we provide them better and faster service.

Customer Focus and Satisfaction

This is by far the most important of the seven Baldrige criteria, accounting for 30 percent of the entire application credits. The foundation is simple: Quality is judged by the customer (client).

As we stated in Chapter 2, "Make no mistake about it, the move toward total quality in our firm is client-driven." Every aspect of our program focuses on improving quality and client service. Even our attention to employee satisfaction is based on the premise that it is key to improved client service.

Have we achieved our goal of improved client service as judged by our clients? We don't have the complete answer yet, but we are confident that we are moving in the right direction. We are still measuring the effects on our clients' satisfaction of the changes we made in our business processes. One thing is certain: The standards against which every person in our organization measures his or her work are clear—quality and client service.

Even our use of technology supports this standard of improving client service. We have several clients who take advantage of direct electronic hookup to our case management system. They no longer incur a charge if they simply want a piece of information or an update on a matter. Our Client Guidelines System was released for use by the firm in 1993. This system stores all of our clients' preferences and requirements in the handling of their files. It is available to everyone with a few keystrokes, and forces us to focus on the quality factors that the clients want.

A Call to Action

One underlying theme of the Baldrige criteria is that you measure your quality achievement not only against internal measurements but also against external benchmarks. Benchmarking is defined as "search for industry best practices that lead to superior performance." It forces a testing of your internal actions against external standards by gathering information to set performance goals based on proven best practices.

In most of the seven criteria listed above, we found nothing for comparison in the legal profession. We had our own data from our client satisfaction and employee surveys, but no basis for comparison. We certainly will continue to survey our clients and employees, but even then, we will not have a competitive benchmark other than our own. We are committed to the process of benchmark gathering and look forward to working with other members of the legal professions in accomplishing this. It is critical that members of the legal profession break down the historical barriers against sharing information with each other and work together to benchmark the profession's best practices. This book is, in many ways, a call to action—Excellence in Action. We believe the legal industry will have to focus its collective energies on how to provide better quality client service and excel in quality management and quality achievement. Then and only then, as the song says, can you change things, and "make this [legal] world a better place if you can."

Making It All Happen

1. After focus groups, there are "new" focus groups. Put together small teams to focus on areas of improvement you would like to address.

2. Our advice: Don't form a committee. They take too much time, are too formal, and tend never to go out of existence. They rarely get the job done. Ad hoc teams are the answer. Meet, solve your problem, get back to work. Give the team the power to implement.

3. Obviously, you are going to want to resurvey to see how you are doing. Review end-of-matter report cards.

4. Redo your action plan and adjust your training to what you have learned.

5. Press your ear to the ground: The hoofbeats of change are out there and will sooner or later be heard. As we observed earlier, we are not sure if the prognosticators and the legal press aren't really the harbinger of change or are fairly accurate predictors of the future course, but we do know that there are a lot of folks reading them and you should, too.

6. Document your problems and address them immediately. Bring quality to the problem-solving process immediately.

7. Review the award criteria for the Malcolm Baldrige National Quality Award. It will give you endless ideas for improvement.

8. Have fun. Have a party, play some Motown hits. For those of you at the authors' age, at the very least, they may bring back fond memories of another time; for a younger generation, they will be introduced to some great music!

TQM in Action

Appendices

Appendix
A

THE ULTIMATE IN BREVITY—HOW TO IMPLEMENT
A TOTAL QUALITY PLAN—IN ONE PAGE

Here in a nutshell is the strategy for implementing a total quality process to improve client service and ultimately client satisfaction.

I.   Who are the leaders in your firm? Once identified, you will need their support for a revolution of change. Educate them on the changing legal services environment and generally on total quality. They will need to focus on client satisfaction. (Chapter 1).

II.   Adopt surveys (first in-house with lawyers *and* support staff, then with clients) as a way to gather data for analysis. Use the results to drive your quality effort and needed changes (Chapter 1).

III.   Identify "change agents" (they are open and flexible thinkers, and leaders) in your organization who are respected and who will be committed to change. Educate and support them. They will be attorneys, support staff, and managers (Chapter 1).

IV.   Develop a systematic plan born out of your survey knowledge that has these elements (at a minimum).

        The "Cornerstones" of Excellence in Action
        • Share a Common Mission and Focus
        • Establish and Teach Quality Standards and Skills
        • Support Substantive Continuing Legal Education
        • Mentor, Monitor, and Measure Results
        • Reward Quality Performance
        • Redefine Quality Service
        • Build Leadership and Teamwork
        • Use Technology to Improve Quality

        Strategize with your change agents on how to present the plan (chapters 2, 3, and 4). Someone must lead the charge and create momentum throughout the *entire* organization.

V.   There will be challenges to your plan. Getting buy-in from some employees will be the biggest hurdle. Learning to communicate effectively in new ways is another (chapters 5 and 6).

VI.   The two most important "Cornerstones" are Mentor, Monitor, and Measure Results and Reward Quality Performance. Are you getting higher quality and seeing improvement? The way to find out is to constantly survey, keep monitoring and measuring, and finally make sure your employee recognition and reward systems are in place and working.

VII.   Training is *the* largest component of what you will do —commit to it in a *big* way. It is essential to improvement. There should be heavy planning and commitment here. Train at *all* levels (chapters 7 and 8).

VIII.   Get ready—do it all again. Start with Point II.

Appendix
B

PLUNKETT & COONEY, P.C.
QUESTIONNAIRE

Thank you in advance for participating in this important survey.

As an employee of the firm, your opinions, ideas and insights are most important to the future of the firm. Please answer the questions as completely as possible. Although the questionnaire is lengthy, we feel that it will be very helpful toward making meaningful changes in the best interest of you the firm and the clients we service. All information will be kept confidential.

1. How do you feel when you tell people you work for Plunkett & Cooney?

    1. ☐   Proud
    2. ☐   Good
    3. ☐   Just a place to work
    4. ☐   Not too happy about telling where I work

2. What do you believe to be the 5 most important aspects of service that clients expect from the firm?

    1. _____
    2. _____
    3. _____
    4. _____
    5. _____

3. What are the 5 most important aspects of your job that should be measured in your performance and recognized in how you are evaluated?

    1. _____
    2. _____
    3. _____
    4. _____
    5. _____

4. Who do you feel is the appropriate person to evaluate your performance? _____

5. With respect to additional training, name 3 non-computer related training topics that you would like to see offered to employees in the next year.

1. _____

2. _____

3. _____

6. If you were the Chief Executive Officer, what would you do to improve the profitability of the firm?

_____

_____

7. What kinds of rewards and recognition would you like to see developed to recognize special or outstanding performance contributions?

_____

_____

8. What do you feel are the three most important changes the firm could make to improve the quality of our client service?

1. _____

2. _____

3. _____

9. Are there existing policies or procedures that you would like to see changed?

1 . ❏ Yes   2. ❏ No

If you answered Yes, please explain.

_____

_____

10. Are the performance evaluations of your work adequate and helpful?

1. ❏   Always
2. ❏   Usually
3. ❏   Seldom
4. ❏   Never

If you answered Seldom or Never, how would you change the evaluation process?

_____

_____

11. Based on your experience in the firm, when "top management" makes a statement concerning future action, can you rely on the statement as a reasonable predictor of things to come?

1. ❏   Always
2. ❏   Usually
3. ❏   Often
4. ❏   Occasionally
5. ❏   Never

If you answered Never or Occasionally, please explain.

_____

_____

12. When you want information or help on a difficult job-related problem, how likely are you to get the help you need?
    1. ☐　　I get no help at all
    2. ☐　　I get very little help
    3. ☐　　I get fairly good help
    4. ☐　　I get all the help I need

13. Do you feel you will be given adequate attention on personal problems if you bring them to the firm's attention?
    1. ☐　　Substantial attention
    2. ☐　　Some attention
    3. ☐　　Not much attention
    4. ☐　　Almost no attention

14. When statements concerning future action (over which they have control) are made by Department Supervisors/ Coordinating Secretaries to whom you are assigned, can you rely on the statement in predicting future action?
    1. ☐　　Always
    2. ☐　　Usually
    3. ☐　　Often
    4. ☐　　Occasionally
    5. ☐　　Never
    If you answered Never or Occasionally, please explain.

_____

_____

15. Does your Attorney/Department Supervisor set a good example in his/her work habits?
    1. ☐　　All of them do
    2. ☐　　Most of them do
    3. ☐　　Some of them do
    4. ☐　　Not very many do
    5. ☐　　None do

16. When you are given new duties and responsibilities, how are they explained?
    1. ☐　　Well explained
    2. ☐　　Adequately explained
    3. ☐　　Partially explained
    4. ☐　　Not satisfactorily explained

17. When changes are made in the work you do, how often are you told the reason for the change?
    1. ☐　　Never
    2. ☐　　Rarely
    3. ☐　　Sometimes
    4. ☐　　Usually
    5. ☐　　Always

18. If assigned to a Coordinating Secretary, does she set a good example in her work habits?

   1. ❑   Never
   2. ❑   Rarely
   3. ❑   Sometimes
   4. ❑   Usually
   5. ❑   Always

If you answered Never or Rarely, please explain.

_____

_____

19. In general, how well do you like your present job?

   1. ❑   I like it very much
   2. ❑   I am satisfied with it
   3. ❑   I neither like nor dislike it
   4. ❑   I dislike it

20. How do you feel about the closeness of supervision of your work by your Attorney/Department Supervisor?

   1. ❑   Generally too close
   2. ❑   Sometimes too close
   3. ❑   About right
   4. ❑   Sometimes not close enough
   5. ❑   Generally not close enough

21. If assigned to a Coordinating Secretary, how do you feel about your working relationship with her?

   1. ❑   Generally too close
   2. ❑   Sometimes too close
   3. ❑   About right
   4. ❑   Sometimes not close enough
   5. ❑   Generally not close enough

22. To what extent are you made to feel that you are really an important part of the firm?

   1. ❑   Not at all
   2. ❑   To a small degree
   3. ❑   To a large degree
   4. ❑   In every way possible

What suggestions do you have in this regard?

_____

_____

23. Does your Attorney/Department Supervisor lead you to feel that you are important to the success of the firm?

   1. ❑   All of them do
   2. ❑   Most of them do
   3. ❑   Some of them do
   4. ❑   None of them do

24. Do you feel that your co-workers are allowed privileges that are not shared by you?

1. ☐ No
2. ☐ Very few
3. ☐ Some
4. ☐ Many

If you answered Many, please explain.

_____

_____

_____

25. Does your Attorney/Department Supervisor consistently provide constructive feedback to you?

1. ☐ Always
2. ☐ Usually
3. ☐ Sometimes
4. ☐ Rarely
5. ☐ Never

26. If assigned to a Coordinating Secretary, does she provide constructive feedback to you in a way that is helpful to you?

1. ☐ Always
2. ☐ Usually
3. ☐ Sometimes
4. ☐ Rarely
5. ☐ Never

If you answered Never or Rarely, please explain.

_____

_____

_____

27. At your performance review, are suggestions and criticisms made in a way which is helpful to you?

1. ☐ Never
2. ☐ Usually
3. ☐ Sometimes
4. ☐ Rarely
5. ☐ Always

28. Are you encouraged by your Attorney/Department Supervisor to offer ideas and suggestions for new or better ways of doing things?

1. ☐ All the time
2. ☐ Often
3. ☐ Sometimes
4. ☐ Rarely
5. ☐ Not at all

29. If assigned to a Coordinating Secretary, does she encourage you to offer ideas and suggestions for new or better ways of doing things?

    1. ☐   All the time
    2. ☐   Often
    3. ☐   Sometimes
    4. ☐   Rarely
    5. ☐   Not at all

30. Are you given adequate information and reasons for new policies, procedures or changes in the firm or your department?

    1. ☐   Always
    2. ☐   Usually
    3. ☐   Sometimes
    4. ☐   Rarely
    5. ☐   Never

31. In your opinion, are the firm's personnel policies fairly and consistently applied?

    1. ☐   All of them are
    2. ☐   Most of them are
    3. ☐   Some of them are
    4. ☐   A few of them are
    5. ☐   None of them are

    If your response is not All of them are, please explain:

    _____

    _____

32. How well does your Attorney/Department Supervisor keep you informed about plans and progress?

    1. ☐   Never
    2. ☐   Seldom
    3. ☐   Sometimes
    4. ☐   Usually
    5. ☐   Always

33. If assigned to a Coordinating Secretary, does she keep you informed about future plans and changes?

    1. ☐   Never
    2. ☐   Seldom
    3. ☐   Sometimes
    4. ☐   Usually
    5. ☐   Always

34. Do you feel that, on the whole, those with whom you work give you the kind of treatment you have a right to expect?

    1. ☐   They all do
    2. ☐   Most of them do
    3. ☐   Some of them do
    4. ☐   Very few of them do
    5. ☐   None of them do

35. How do you feel about the assistance you receive from other employees in the firm?

    1. ☐   I get all the help I need
    2. ☐   I get some help
    3. ☐   I get very little help
    4. ☐   I get no help at all

If you have answered I get no help at all, what suggestions do you have?

_____

_____

_____

36. When you have a complaint, how is it handled?

    1. ☐   It is handled well
    2. ☐   Some effort is made, but not enough
    3. ☐   Complaints are poorly handled
    4. ☐   I never have a complaint

37. How knowledgeable about your work is your Attorney/Department Supervisor?

    1. ☐   A real expert in the work we do
    2. ☐   Handles most problems well
    3. ☐   Knows just enough to get by
    4. ☐   Doesn't know much about the work

38. How skillful is your Attorney/Department Supervisor in helping you deal with the needs and problems of people in your firm?

    1. ☐   A good leader—knows how to take care of people
    2. ☐   Does a fair job of handling our problems
    3. ☐   Doesn't know what to do when we have a problem
    4. ☐   Doesn't really care about our problems

39. If assigned to a Coordinating Secretary, how skillful is she in helping you and others deal with the problems you encounter in your daily work?

    1. ☐   A good leader—knows how to take care of people
    2. ☐   Does a fair job of handling our problems
    3. ☐   Doesn't know what to do when we have a problem
    4. ☐   Doesn't really care about our problems

40. Do you think you have a good understanding of the following (write yes or no):

_____Pension Plan	_____Vacation Policy
_____Disability Policy	_____Open Door Policy
_____Profit Sharing	_____401K Plan
_____Personal Time	_____Health Care Insurance/Blue Cross
_____Blue Cross	_____Dental Compensation System

41. How do you think the firm's benefit plans compare to those of similar size firms?

    1. ☐   Better than most
    2. ☐   About the same
    3. ☐   Not as good as most

42. Of the benefits that you are currently receiving, please indicate those that are most and least important to you:

    Rank them 1-8, with 1 being Most Important and 8 being Least Important.

    _____Pension Plan

    _____Vacation Policy

    _____Disability Policy

    _____Open Door Policy

    _____Profit Sharing

    _____401K Plan

    _____Personal Time

    _____Health Care Insurance/Blue Cross

    _____Blue Cross

    _____Dental Compensation System

43. If the firm has the opportunity to offer alternative benefits, which would be the most important to you?

    Indicate your top 5 selections, 1-5, with 1 being the highest.

    _____Vision Care

    _____Educational Assistance/Tuition Refunds/Loans

    _____Child Care

    _____Medical Care Reimbursement

    _____Child Care Reimbursement

    _____Dependent Care Reimbursement

    _____Other

44. Do you understand how medical/child care reimbursement allowance accounts work?

    1. ☐ Yes   2. ☐ No

45. Would you be willing to contribute to additional benefits if you were to incur a tax advantage or group cost savings?

    1. ☐ Yes   2. ☐ No

46. How important is the current benefit package to your job satisfaction?

    1. ☐   Very important
    2. ☐   Important
    3. ☐   Not important

47. Would you be interested in a cafeteria or flexible benefits program where employees would have the opportunity to select their benefits from a group of benefits? Each employee would be allowed a defined dollar amount of benefits (Please print your answer.)

_____

_____

_____

48. What problems do you have with the physical facilities in which you work? (Please print your answer.)

_____

_____

_____

49. To what extent does the firm have a real interest in the welfare and happiness of those who work here?
   1. ☐   To a very little extent
   2. ☐   To a little extent
   3. ☐   To some extent
   4. ☐   To a great extent
   5. ☐   To a very great extent

50. To what extent does the firm have clear-cut, reasonable goals and objectives?
   1. ☐   To a very little extent
   2. ☐   To a little extent
   3. ☐   To some extent
   4. ☐   To a great extent
   5. ☐   To a very great extent

51. To what extent do you have a feeling of loyalty toward the firm?
   1. ☐   To a very little extent
   2. ☐   To a little extent
   3. ☐   To some extent
   4. ☐   To a great extent
   5. ☐   To a very great extent

52. How are differences and disagreements between co-workers handled in the firm?
   1. ☐   Disagreements are almost always ignored
   2. ☐   Disagreements are often ignored
   3. ☐   Sometimes disagreements are accepted and worked through; sometimes they are ignored
   4. ☐   Disagreements are usually accepted as necessary and desirable and worked through
   5. ☐   Disagreements are almost always accepted as necessary and desirable and are worked through

53. All in all, how satisfied are you with your co-workers?
   1. ☐   Very dissatisfied
   2 ☐   Somewhat dissatisfied
   3. ☐   Neither satisfied nor dissatisfied
   4. ☐   Fairly satisfied
   5. ☐   Satisfied

54. All in all, how satisfied are you with your Attorney/Department Supervisor?

1. ☐   Very dissatisfied
2 ☐   Somewhat dissatisfied
3. ☐   Neither satisfied nor dissatisfied
4. ☐   Fairly satisfied
5. ☐   Satisfied

55. If assigned to a Coordinating Secretary, how satisfied are you with her?

1. ☐   Very dissatisfied
2 ☐   Somewhat dissatisfied
3. ☐   Neither satisfied nor dissatisfied
4. ☐   Fairly satisfied
5. ☐   Satisfied

56. All in all, how satisfied are you with your job?

1. ☐   Very dissatisfied
2 ☐   Somewhat dissatisfied
3. ☐   Neither satisfied nor dissatisfied
4. ☐   Fairly satisfied
5. ☐   Satisfied

57. To what extent do you enjoy performing the actual day-today activities that make up your job?

1. ☐   Not at all
2. ☐   To a little extent
3. ☐   To some extent
4. ☐   To a great extent
5. ☐   To a very great extent

58. How much do you look forward to coming to work each day?

1. ☐   To a very great extent
2. ☐   To a great extent
3. ☐   To some extent
4. ☐   To a little extent
5. ☐   Not at all

59. To what extent are there things about working for the firm (people, policies, or conditions) that encourage you to work hard?

1. ☐   To a very great extent
2. ☐   To a great extent
3. ☐   To some extent
4. ☐   To a little extent
5. ☐   Not at all

60. To what extent do you feel your pay is related to how much you help the firm be successful?

    1. ☐ Not at all
    2. ☐ To a little extent
    3. ☐ To some extent
    4. ☐ To a great extent
    5. ☐ To a very great extent

61. How are goals set in the firm?

    1. ☐ Goals are announced with no chance to raise questions or give comments
    2. ☐ Goals are announced and explained, and chance is given to ask questions
    3. ☐ Goals are made up, but are discussed with employees and sometimes change before being used
    4. ☐ Different alternative goals are made up by the supervisor, and employees are asked to discuss them and say which they think is best
    5. ☐ Problems are presented to those employees who are involved, and the goals felt to be best are then set by the employees and supervisors together

62. To what extent are decisions made at the right levels in the firm?

    1. ☐ Not at all
    2. ☐ To a little extent
    3. ☐ To some extent
    4. ☐ To a great extent
    5. ☐ To a very great extent

63. When decisions are being made, to what extent are the persons affected asked for their ideas?

    1. ☐ Not at all
    2. ☐ To a little extent
    3. ☐ To some extent
    4. ☐ To a great extent
    5. ☐ To a very great extent

64. People at all levels in the firm may have information about how to do things better. To what extent do you feel such information at all levels is used?

    1. ☐ Not at all
    2. ☐ To a little extent
    3. ☐ To some extent
    4. ☐ To a great extent
    5. ☐ To a very great extent

65. To what extent do different sections/departments plan their work activities with one another?

    1. ☐ Not at all
    2. ☐ To a little extent
    3. ☐ To some extent
    4. ☐ To a great extent
    5. ☐ To a very great extent

For the following set of items: Please read each question and then answer both for how it is now, and for how you would like it to be.

How friendly and easy to approach is your Attorney/Department Supervisor?

66. This is how it is now:
   1. ☐   To a very little extent
   2. ☐   To a little extent
   3. ☐   To some extent
   4. ☐   To a great extent
   5. ☐   To a very great extent

67. This is how I would like it to be:
   1. ☐   To a very little extent
   2. ☐   To a little extent
   3. ☐   To some extent
   4. ☐   To a great extent
   5. ☐   To a very great extent

If assigned, how friendly and easy to approach is your Coordinating Secretary?

68. This is how it is now:
   1. ☐   To a very little extent
   2. ☐   To a little extent
   3. ☐   To some extent
   4. ☐   To a great extent
   5. ☐   To a very great extent

69. This is how I would like it to be:
   1. ☐   To a very little extent
   2. ☐   To a little extent
   3. ☐   To some extent
   4. ☐   To a great extent
   5. ☐   To a very great extent

When you talk with your Attorney/Department Supervisor, to what extent does he/she pay attention to what you are saying?

70. This is how it is now:
   1. ☐   To a very little extent
   2. ☐   To a little extent
   3. ☐   To some extent
   4. ☐   To a great extent
   5. ☐   To a very great extent

71. This is how I would like it to be:
   1. ☐   To a very little extent
   2. ☐   To a little extent
   3. ☐   To some extent
   4. ☐   To a great extent
   5. ☐   To a very great extent

To what extent is your Attorney/Department Supervisor willing to listen to your problems?

72. This is how it is now:
    1. ☐   To a very little extent
    2. ☐   To a little extent
    3. ☐   To some extent
    4. ☐   To a great extent
    5. ☐   To a very great extent

73. This is how I would like it to be:
    1. ☐   To a very little extent
    2. ☐   To a little extent
    3. ☐   To some extent
    4. ☐   To a great extent
    5. ☐   To a very great extent

How much does your Attorney/Department Supervisor encourage people to give their best effort?

74. This is how it is now:
    1. ☐   To a very little extent
    2. ☐   To a little extent
    3. ☐   To some extent
    4. ☐   To a great extent
    5. ☐   To a very great extent

75. This is how I would like it to be:
    1. ☐   To a very little extent
    2. ☐   To a little extent
    3. ☐   To some extent
    4. ☐   To a great extent
    5. ☐   To a very great extent

To what extent does your Attorney/Department Supervisor maintain high standards of performance?

76. This is how it is now:
    1. ☐   To a very little extent
    2. ☐   To a little extent
    3. ☐   To some extent
    4. ☐   To a great extent
    5. ☐   To a very great extent

77. This is how I would like it to be:
    1. ☐   To a very little extent
    2. ☐   To a little extent
    3. ☐   To some extent
    4. ☐   To a great extent
    5. ☐   To a very great extent

To what extent does your Attorney/Department Supervisor show you how to improve your performance?

78. This is how it is now:
1. ☐ To a very little extent
2. ☐ To a little extent
3. ☐ To some extent
4. ☐ To a great extent
5. ☐ To a very great extent

79. This is how I would like it to be:
1. ☐ To a very little extent
2. ☐ To a little extent
3. ☐ To some extent
4. ☐ To a great extent
5. ☐ To a very great extent

To what extent does your Attorney/Department supervisor encourage people who work for her/him to exchange opinions and ideas?

80. This is how it is now:
1. ☐ To a very little extent
2. ☐ To a little extent
3. ☐ To some extent
4. ☐ To a great extent
5. ☐ To a very great extent

81. This is how I would like it to be:
1. ☐ To a very little extent
2. ☐ To a little extent
3. ☐ To some extent
4. ☐ To a great extent
5. ☐ To a very great extent

82. To what extent do you feel your Attorney/Department Supervisor has confidence and trust in you?
1. ☐ To a very little extent
2. ☐ To a little extent
3. ☐ To some extent
4. ☐ To a great extent
5. ☐ To a very great extent

83. To what extent do you have confidence and trust in your Attorney/Department Supervisor?
1. ☐ To a very little extent
2. ☐ To a little extent
3. ☐ To some extent
4. ☐ To a great extent
5. ☐ To a very great extent

84. If assigned to a Coordinating Secretary, do you have confidence and trust in her?

1. ☐ Not at all
2. ☐ To a little extent
3. ☐ To some extent
4. ☐ To a great extent
5. ☐ To a very great extent

How friendly and easy is it to approach your co-workers?

85. This is how it is now:

1. ☐ To a very little extent
2. ☐ To a little extent
3. ☐ To some extent
4. ☐ To a great extent
5. ☐ To a very great extent

86. This is how I would like it to be:

1. ☐ To a very little extent
2. ☐ To a little extent
3. ☐ To some extent
4. ☐ To a great extent
5. ☐ To a very great extent

When you talk with co-workers, to what extent do they pay attention to what you are saying?

87. This is how it is now:

1. ☐ To a very little extent
2. ☐ To a little extent
3. ☐ To some extent
4. ☐ To a great extent
5. ☐ To a very great extent

88. This is how I would like it to be:

1. ☐ To a very little extent
2. ☐ To a little extent
3. ☐ To some extent
4. ☐ To a great extent
5. ☐ To a very great extent

To what extent are co-workers willing to listen to your problems?

89. This is how it is now:

1. ☐ To a very little extent
2. ☐ To a little extent
3. ☐ To some extent
4. ☐ To a great extent
5. ☐ To a very great extent

90. This is how I would like it to be:
1. ☐ To a very little extent
2. ☐ To a little extent
3. ☐ To some extent
4. ☐ To a great extent
5. ☐ To a very great extent

How much do co-workers encourage each other to give their best effort?

91. This is how it is now:
1. ☐ To a very little extent
2. ☐ To a little extent
3. ☐ To some extent
4. ☐ To a great extent
5. ☐ To a very great extent

92. This is how I would like it to be:
1. ☐ To a very little extent
2. ☐ To a little extent
3. ☐ To some extent
4. ☐ To a great extent
5. ☐ To a very great extent

To what extent do co-workers maintain high standards of performance?

93. This is how it is now:
1. ☐ To a very little extent
2. ☐ To a little extent
3. ☐ To some extent
4. ☐ To a great extent
5. ☐ To a very great extent

94. This is how I would like it to be:
1. ☐ To a very little extent
2. ☐ To a little extent
3. ☐ To some extent
4. ☐ To a great extent
5. ☐ To a very great extent

To what extent do co-workers help you find ways to do a better job?

95. This is how it is now:
1. ☐ To a very little extent
2. ☐ To a little extent
3. ☐ To some extent
4. ☐ To a great extent
5. ☐ To a very great extent

96. This is how I would like it to be:
    1. ☐ To a very little extent
    2. ☐ To a little extent
    3. ☐ To some extent
    4. ☐ To a great extent
    5. ☐ To a very great extent

To what extent do co-workers offer each other new ideas for solving job-related problems?

97. This is how it is now:
    1. ☐ To a very little extent
    2. ☐ To a little extent
    3. ☐ To some extent
    4. ☐ To a great extent
    5. ☐ To a very great extent

98. This is how I would like it to be:
    1. ☐ To a very little extent
    2. ☐ To a little extent
    3. ☐ To some extent
    4. ☐ To a great extent
    5. ☐ To a very great extent

How much do co-workers encourage each other to work as a team?

99. This is how it is now:
    1. ☐ To a very little extent
    2. ☐ To a little extent
    3. ☐ To some extent
    4. ☐ To a great extent
    5. ☐ To a very great extent

100. This is how I would like it to be:
    1. ☐ To a very little extent
    2. ☐ To a little extent
    3. ☐ To some extent
    4. ☐ To a great extent
    5. ☐ To a very great extent

How much do co-workers emphasize goals?

101. This is how it is now:
    1. ☐ To a very little extent
    2. ☐ To a little extent
    3. ☐ To some extent
    4. ☐ To a great extent
    5. ☐ To a very great extent

102. This is how I would like it to be:
   1. ☐   To a very little extent
   2. ☐   To a little extent
   3. ☐   To some extent
   4. ☐   To a great extent
   5. ☐   To a very great extent

To what extent do co-workers exchange opinions and ideas?

103. This is how it is now:
   1. ☐   To a very little extent
   2. ☐   To a little extent
   3. ☐   To some extent
   4. ☐   To a great extent
   5. ☐   To a very great extent

104. This is how I would like it to be:
   1. ☐   To a very little extent
   2. ☐   To a little extent
   3. ☐   To some extent
   4. ☐   To a great extent
   5. ☐   To a very great extent

105. To what extent do your co-workers make good decisions and solve problems well?
   1. ☐   To a very little extent
   2. ☐   To a little extent
   3. ☐   To some extent
   4. ☐   To a great extent
   5. ☐   To a very great extent

106. To what extent do your co-workers know what their jobs are and know how to do them well?
   1. ☐   To a very little extent
   2. ☐   To a little extent
   3. ☐   To some extent
   4. ☐   To a great extent
   5. ☐   To a very great extent

107. To what extent do your co-workers share information about important events?
   1. ☐   To a very little extent
   2. ☐   To a little extent
   3. ☐   To some extent
   4. ☐   To a great extent
   5. ☐   To a very great extent

108. To what extent do you have confidence and trust in your co-workers?
   1. ☐   To a very little extent
   2. ☐   To a little extent
   3. ☐   To some extent
   4. ☐   To a great extent
   5. ☐   To a very great extent

109. To what extent are the equipment and tools you use adequate to perform the job?
    1. ☐ To a very little extent
    2. ☐ To a little extent
    3. ☐ To some extent
    4. ☐ To a great extent
    5. ☐ To a very great extent

    Please explain: (Please print your answer.)

    _____

    _____

    _____

110. To what extent do the equipment and tools you use, improve your efficiency?
    1. ☐ To a very little extent
    2. ☐ To a little extent
    3. ☐ To some extent
    4. ☐ To a great extent
    5. ☐ To a very great extent

    Please explain: (Please print your answer.)

    _____

    _____

    _____

111. To what extent are the equipment and tools you have to do your work with well-maintained?
    1. ☐ To a very little extent
    2. ☐ To a little extent
    3. ☐ To some extent
    4. ☐ To a great extent
    5. ☐ To a very great extent

    Please explain: (Please print your answer.)

    _____

    _____

    _____

112. To what extent do you feel a real responsibility to help the firm be successful?
    1. ☐ To a very little extent
    2. ☐ To a little extent
    3. ☐ To some extent
    4. ☐ To a great extent
    5. ☐ To a very great extent

113. Do you feel that you are properly compensated for the work you perform?

    1. ❏ Yes   2. ❏ No

    Please explain either answer.

    _____

    _____

    _____

114. To what extent do you feel that your firm's image could be improved?

    1. ❏   To a very little extent
    2. ❏   To a little extent
    3. ❏   To some extent
    4. ❏   To a great extent
    5. ❏   To a very great extent

    Please explain: (Please print your answer.)

    _____

    _____

    _____

115. Is your firm work atmosphere (i.e., positive, professional, conscientious) conducive to the type of services provided?

    1. ❏   Always
    2. ❏   Usually
    3. ❏   Often
    4. ❏   Occasionally
    5. ❏   Never

    If you answered Never, please explain.

    _____

    _____

    _____

116. If you had the decision to make, what one single change would you make as it relates to your job? (Please print your answer.)

    _____

    _____

    _____

117. How could your work and/or your department's work group be improved? What changes would you make if you had the authority and responsibility? (Please print your answer.)

    _____

    _____

    _____

118. Do you meet with any obstructions in your work? If so, what are they?

_____

_____

_____

119. How do you communicate your ideas for changes/improvements to the firm?

_____

_____

_____

120. What ideas do you have for improving the firm?

_____

_____

_____

121. Please discuss any areas that were not covered in this questionnaire that you feel are important to you.

_____

_____

_____

122. Would you be interested in participating in a focus group to discuss ideas related to developing a performance appraisal and incentive bonus program?

1. ☐ Yes   2. ☐ No

123. How many years have you been with the firm? _____

SIGNATURE _____

POSITION _____

DATE _____

Please place completed survey in the attached envelope and seal it. Then forward it to the Mailroom. The sealed envelopes will be forwarded to the Human Resource Department.

Appendix
C

PLUNKETT & COONEY ATTORNEY SURVEY

Name: _____

Section: _____

YOUR PRACTICE

1. What are your practice areas (list them by percentage of practice in descending order)?

2. What are your practice strengths?

3. Describe legal services you provide that are unique and cannot be obtained anywhere else in your service area.

4. What are your practice weaknesses?

5. Describe three short-term goals for your practice in 1994.

6. Describe three long-term (3- to 5-year) goals for your practice.

7.   Who are your competitors?

8.   Review the client list; what clients have the greatest potential for more business?

9.   What cross-selling can be done?

10.   What new clients have you obtained in the last year?

11.   Describe how the business was obtained and its nature.

12.   What clients have you lost in the last year?

13.   Describe how the client was lost and the nature of its business.

14.   What referrals have you made this year?

15.   What referrals from practicing attorneys have you received this year?

SECTION PRACTICE

16. What are the practice areas covered by your section?

17. What are the practice strengths of your section?

18. Describe legal services your section provides that are unique and cannot be obtained anywhere else in its service area.

19. What are the practice weaknesses of your section?

20. Describe three short-term (1 year) goals for your section in 1994.

21. Describe three long-term (3 to 5 year) goals for your section.

22. Who are your section's competitors?

23. Review the Section Client List; what clients have the greatest potential for more business?

24. What cross-selling can be done with other sections?

25. What new clients have been obtained by the section in the last year?

26. Describe how the business was obtained and its nature.

27. What clients has the section lost in the last year?

28. Describe how the client was lost and the nature of its business.

FIRM PRACTICE

29. How would you describe the business of Plunkett & Cooney?

30. What are Plunkett & Cooney's strengths?

31. Describe legal services that Plunkett & Cooney provides that are unique and cannot be obtained anywhere else in its service area.

32. What are Plunkett & Cooney's weaknesses?

33. Describe three short-term (1-year) goals for Plunkett & Cooney in 1994.

34. Describe three long-term (3- to 5-year) goals for Plunkett & Cooney.

35. Who are the firm's competitors?

36. Review the Firm Client List; what clients have the greatest potential for more business?

37. What cross-selling can be done?

38. What new clients have been obtained by the firm last year?

39. Recall how the business was obtained and its nature.

40. What clients has the firm lost in the last year?

41. Describe how the client was lost and the nature of its business.

42. Please score these factors for the firm.
    1 represents a low rating - 5 represents a high rating.

Technical Expertise	5	4	3	2	1
Service	5	4	3	2	1
Responsiveness	5	4	3	2	1
Fee Structure	5	4	3	2	1
Legal Community Reputation	5	4	3	2	1
Competitiveness vs. other Firms	5	4	3	2	1
Business Community Reputation	5	4	3	2	1
Political Contacts	5	4	3	2	1
Business/Community Presence	5	4	3	2	1
Social/Community Presence	5	4	3	2	1
Firm Management and Governance	5	4	3	2	1
Marketing	5	4	3	2	1
Salary and Bonus System	5	4	3	2	1
Associate Support	5	4	3	2	1
Continuing Legal Education	5	4	3	2	1
Internal Communication	5	4	3	2	1
Work Environment	5	4	3	2	1
Sense of Teamwork	5	4	3	2	1
Training	5	4	3	2	1
Firm Growth	5	4	3	2	1

Add Comments Below:

43. Please score these practice areas.
    1 represents a low rating - 5 represents a high rating.

Appeals & Research	5	4	3	2	1
Architects & Engineering Liab	5	4	3	2	1
Automobile Liability	5	4	3	2	1
Aviation Law	5	4	3	2	1
Banking & Finance	5	4	3	2	1
Bankruptcy	5	4	3	2	1
Business Litigation	5	4	3	2	1
Computer Law	5	4	3	2	1
Construction Law	5	4	3	2	1
Corporate, Tax & Business Law	5	4	3	2	1
Criminal Law & White Collar Crime	5	4	3	2	1
Drug Liability	5	4	3	2	1
Entertainment & Sports Law	5	4	3	2	1
Environmental Law	5	4	3	2	1
Family Law	5	4	3	2	1
Franchising	5	4	3	2	1
Health Care Law	5	4	3	2	1
Hospital Law	5	4	3	2	1
Insurance Law	5	4	3	2	1

International Law	5	4	3	2	1
Labor & Employment Law	5	4	3	2	1
Legislative Affairs	5	4	3	2	1
Liquor Liability Law	5	4	3	2	1
Litigation Support Systems	5	4	3	2	1
Medical Malpractice Defense	5	4	3	2	1
Municipal Finance Law	5	4	3	2	1
Municipal Law	5	4	3	2	1
No Fault Law	5	4	3	2	1
Premises Liability	5	4	3	2	1
Probate & Estate Planning	5	4	3	2	1
Products Liability	5	4	3	2	1
Professional Liability	5	4	3	2	1
Property Loss	5	4	3	2	1
Real Property Law	5	4	3	2	1
Regulatory & Administrative Law	5	4	3	2	1
Worker's Compensation	5	4	3	2	1

44. What practice areas have the greatest potential for growth?

45. What areas of expertise should be added to the firm?

46. Please score these activities.
    Five is valuable, One is not valuable.

Surveys:

Client Satisfaction Surveys	5	4	3	2	1

Public Speaking:

Bar Related Groups	5	4	3	2	1
Business & Industry Groups	5	4	3	2	1
Civic Groups	5	4	3	2	1

Memberships:

Bar Related Groups	5	4	3	2	1
Business & Industry Groups	5	4	3	2	1
Charities	5	4	3	2	1
Civic Groups	5	4	3	2	1
Country/Boat Clubs	5	4	3	2	1

Seminars:

Sole Sponsor	5	4	3	2	1
As Co-Sponsor	5	4	3	2	1

Brochures:

Firm	5	4	3	2	1
Section	5	4	3	2	1
Robert E. Rutt Advocacy Center	5	4	3	2	1

Newsletters:

Communicator	5	4	3	2	1
In Summary	5	4	3	2	1
Insurance Section	5	4	3	2	1
Macomb County Office	5	4	3	2	1

Publishing:

Legal Newspapers	5	4	3	2	1
Business or Industry Magazines	5	4	3	2	1
Books or Treatises	5	4	3	2	1

Public Relations Activities:

Press Releases	5	4	3	2	1

Marketing Activities:

Marketing Committee	5	4	3	2	1
Firm Marketing Plan	5	4	3	2	1
Section Marketing Plans	5	4	3	2	1
Individual Marketing Plans	5	4	3	2	1
RFP Responses	5	4	3	2	1

Add Comments Below:

47. How is our fee structure viewed in the marketplace?

48. Which clients should be approached about a rate increase this year?

49. Which clients should not be approached about a rate increase this year?

50. What obstacles or barriers are there to providing outstanding legal service to clients?

Appendix
D

REQUEST FOR PROPOSAL CLIENT SATISFACTION SURVEY

Objective:

Plunkett & Cooney, P.C. is a law firm of approximately 130 attorneys with seven Michigan offices, a Washington, D.C. office, a Pittsburgh office and affiliates in Toronto, Ontario, and London, England. We have a client base of approximately 3,500 insurance companies, corporations, health care facilities and individuals. Plunkett & Cooney, P.C. is requesting proposals from competent and qualified analysts to provide a third party independent client satisfaction survey that will maintain the confidentiality of our clients.

Scope of Services:

This survey will be accomplished in one of four ways: by executive interview, by written survey, by telephone survey, or by all of the above. Once the survey is completed, an in-depth analysis of the results is to be provided.

Requirements:

1. Knowledge of the legal services field.

2. Ability to complete the survey and the analysis by our firm deadline.

3. Provide a sample of a customized written survey and sample telephone survey and an explanation of the procedures you would use to conduct each.

4. Ability to provide an in-depth analysis and summary of the survey results.

5. Provide recommendations regarding what action to take.

6. Provide briefing sessions to various sections of the firm on the survey results.

7. Provide a breakdown of your billing procedure detailing how costs will be charged with an estimated total cost for the project, on a not to exceed basis.

8. Provide six copies of your proposal.

LEGAL CLIENT SATISFACTION
TELEPHONE SURVEY

Hello, I'm _____ calling from Market Strategies, Inc. in Livonia. We were hired by Plunkett & Cooney to conduct a survey of their clients to find out how satisfied they are with the legal services they are receiving. Would you be able to answer some questions at this time? All interviews are strictly confidential.

Thinking about your entire relationship with Plunkett & Cooney...

1. Using a zero-to-ten scale, with ten meaning extremely satisfied and zero meaning extremely dissatisfied; How would you rate your SATISFACTION with the legal services Plunkett & Cooney have provided for you? You may use any number from zero to ten.

2. Does your company currently use other law firms as well as Plunkett & Cooney, or strictly Plunkett & Cooney?

3. (If 2=yes) Approximately what percent of your company's legal work goes to Plunkett & Cooney? Would you say less than 25%, 25% to 50%, 50% to 75% or more than 75%?

4. For what reasons do you choose to use Plunkett & Cooney? (OPEN END).

5. Compared to other law firms, would you say that Plunkett & Cooney's overall legal services are better, worse, or basically the same?

Now, let's talk about how you communicate with Plunkett & Cooney...

6. How would you describe the quality of your communication with Plunkett & Cooney?
   A. Very clear/No problems
   B. Occasional miscommunications and misunderstandings
   C. Somewhat frequent lapses in communication
   D. Regular and repeated communication problems

7. What comes to mind as an example of a communication problem you had last year with Plunkett & Cooney? (OPEN END)

8. Again, using the same zero-to-ten scale, with ten meaning extremely clear and understandable and zero meaning not clear at all; How would you describe the clarity of the bills you receive from Plunkett & Cooney?

9. What do you think Plunkett & Cooney could do to make their billing process clearer and easier to understand? (OPEN END)

10. How long has your company been using Plunkett & Cooney's services?
    A. Less than one year
    B. 1-3 years
    C. 3-5 years
    D. 5-10 years
    E. More than 10 years

Now I am going to read you a number of situations which could have occurred over the course of your relationship with any law firm. For each one, please tell me how often this situation has ACTUALLY OCCURRED during your relationship with Plunkett & Cooney. Please use a zero to ten scale for each answer; zero meaning the situation has NEVER happened, and ten meaning it happens ALL THE TIME. You may use any number between zero and ten.

(RANDOMIZE)

11. Billed for service that tends to "reinvent the wheel".

12. Received a deposition summary, or other types of analysis which went on at a greater length than necessary.

13. Had a sense that your attorney really understood what you need to do your job better.

14. Dealt with an attorney who was actively working to reduce costs.

15. Questioned the competence of an attorney working for you.

16. Billed for research when working with an attorney on a standard problem.

17. Received unnecessary letters, with no substantive content.

18. Provided you with an early and accurate evaluation of your case.

19. Billed for work not authorized.

20. Received regular, clear and concise communication.

For each one of the following service characteristics, please rate how well Plunkett & Cooney attorneys meet your expectations. Use a zero-to-ten scale where zero means they FALL SHORT of your expectations and ten means they EXCEED your expectations; and five means they MEET your expectations.

(RANDOMIZE)

21. Being available to answer legal questions when you call.

22. Knowledgeable and competent in their specific legal specialty.

23. Knowing what is essential and what is not essential.

24. Providing clear, concise, and readable reports.

25. Delivering work in a timely manner.

26. Taking the time to explain things to you clearly.

27. Following up with you when they promise they will; i.e. returns phone calls promptly.

28. Not being distracted by other clients and projects when they are working with you.

29. Giving an early and accurate evaluation of cases.

30. Striving to make it easier to do business with Plunkett & Cooney.

31. Always know what attorney is responsible for your file.

Thinking more specifically about types of legal services...

Now I am going to read you a list of different legal services which Plunkett & Cooney provides. For each one, please tell me if you have used this service. (IF DON'T USE NOW, ASK:) How INTERESTED do you think you will be in using this service in the future; very interested, somewhat interested, not very interested or not interested at all.

(RANDOMIZE)

32. Appeals/Research

33. Business Litigation

34. Corporate & Banking Transactions

35. Labor, Employment Law

36. Workers Compensation Litigation

37. General Liability

38. Legislative Affairs

39. Municipal Law

40. Insurance Law

41. Medical Liability

42. Products Liability

43. Professional Liability

44. Environmental Law

45. Entertainment/Sports Law

46. Real Estate Law

47. Family Law

Now, I am going to read you a list of Plunkett & Cooney's different branch offices. For each one, please tell me if you were aware of the branch office. (IF NOT AWARE, ASK:) How INTERESTED do you think you will be in using this branch office in the future; very interested, somewhat interested, not very interested or not interested at all.

48. Pittsburgh

49. Bloomfield Hills

50. Mt. Clemens

51. Lansing

52. Petoskey

53. Flint

54. Kalamazoo

55. Considering your company's needs, where would it be most helpful to locate a Plunkett & Cooney new branch office in this state or in the midwest? (OPEN END)

56. What legal services do you anticipate that you will need in the next 5 years?

57. Do you perceive that Plunkett & Cooney will provide these services?

Now, just two final questions about billing...

58. How satisfied are you with Plunkett & Cooney's current fee structure? Would you say very satisfied, somewhat satisfied, somewhat dissatisfied, or very dissatisfied.

59. Compared to other firms that you use, would you say Plunkett & Cooney's fees are; below average, average or above average.

CONFIDENTIAL QUESTIONNAIRE

Thank you for taking the time to complete this short questionnaire concerning your relationship with Plunkett & Cooney. Please be as honest as possible in your answers; all responses will be held completely confidential. You need not include your name on this page. When you have completed the questionnaire, please send it to Market Strategies, Inc., using the enclosed return envelope.

Please circle the appropriate responses.

1. Considering your entire relationship with Plunkett & Cooney over the time you have been a client, how would you rate you SATISFACTION with services Plunkett & Cooney have provided for you? Please circle your answer using the zero-to-ten scale below; zero means not at all satisfied and ten means extremely satisfied.

    0   1   2   3   4   5   6   7   8   9   10

2. Overall, how consistent is the service you have received from Plunkett & Cooney? Please circle your answer using the zero-to-ten scale below; zero means not at all satisfied and ten means extremely satisfied.

    0   1   2   3   4   5   6   7   8   9   10

3. How would you describe the quality of your communication with Plunkett & Cooney?

    1   Very clear/No problems
    2   Occasional miscommunications and misunderstandings
    3   Somewhat frequent lapses in communication
    4   Regular and repeated communication problems

4. What comes to mind as an example of a communication problem you had last year with Plunkett & Cooney (WRITE IN RESPONSE)

5. For how long have you engaged the services of Plunkett & Cooney?

    1   Less than one year
    2   1-3 years
    3   3-5 years
    4   5-10 years
    5   More than 10 years

Appendix
E

PRESENTATION SLIDES

Outline for a Total Quality Program

res ipsa
loquitur

Tempus Fugit

CARPE DIEM

mundi cani

Ipso Facto

Time Flies

Tempus Fugi

Times have changed
Legal Marketplace is different

EXCELLENTIA IN ACTIONE

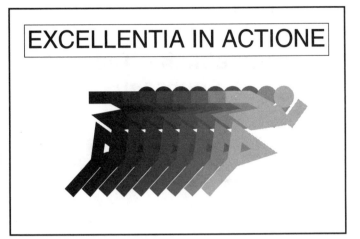

EXCELLENCE IN ACTION

A Practical Guide to Total Quality -- the "Plunkett & Cooney" Way

---

Establish a Total Quality Program
Revitalize a "Plunkett & Cooney Way"
Redefine Client Service
Establish a Team Approach

To Establish a Total Quality Program
We Must Recognize

Prime Responsibility is on Firm Leadership

Must involve every Person in the Firm

Based on Clients' Perceptions & Expectations

Depends on Individual, Team and Firm Performance

Establish a Total Quality Program

Redefine Client Service

Improve our listening skills

Improve our understanding of client needs

Client Service is more than a favorable verdict.

E I A

Redefine Client Service

Establish a Team Approach

E I A

Rejuvenate the Section System

Establish Teams for each Matter
Shareholder
Associate
Paralegal
PSS

Better Define Roles & Responsibilities

Learn to Delegate

E I A

Establish a Team Approach

Understand Clients' Expectations
Define Plunkett & Cooney Standards
Demonstrate (Teach) Standards
Integrate, Monitor and Reinforce Standards
Measure Commitment to Quality
Reward Commitment to Quality

E I A

Review Detroit Market Survey

Conduct Comprehensive Client Survey

Utilize Client Guidelines Database

Develop "Engagement Letters"

Implement End of Matter "Report Cards"

E I A

Understand Clients' Expectations

Integrate Known Standards into Client Guidelines Database

Develop Work Product / Brief Bank Database

Utilize "Action Plans" in File Handling

E I A

Define Plunkett & Cooney Standards

Conduct Integrated EIA Training

Schedule a Leadership Training Program for Section Leaders

Offer On-Going Training in Management and Communication Skills

E I A

Demonstrate (Teach) Standards

Establish an Associate Mentoring Program

Implement a Quality Assurance and Peer Review Program

Realign Coordinating Secretaries with Sections

Regular Section Leader Meetings

E I A

Integrate, Monitor & Reinforce Standards

Revise Attorney Performance Evaluation

Revise Paralegal Performance Evaluation

Revise PSS Performance Evaluation

Continue to Integrate Performance Evaluations into our Compensation System

E I A

Measure & Reward Commitment

Making it Happen

Revamp our Training Program

New Series to begin in September
Parallel Series for Attorneys, Paralegals & Staff

Excellence in Action Series
Establish and Teach Quality Standards
Focus on Office Management and File Handling

Using Technology Series
Improve Computer Skills
Emphasize Access to Firm-Wide Knowledge

EXCELLENCE IN ACTION - ATTORNEY SERIES

Managing Your Office
Professionalism & Business Ethics
Billing Guidelines & Procedures
Managing the Client Relationship
Managing Your Files
Managing the Attorney/Staff Relationship
Preparation of Pleadings
Getting Assistance - Internal & External
Time Management
Stress Management

USING TECHNOLOGY - ATTORNEY SERIES

Phones, Phone Mail, Faxes & Equitrac
Word Processing I & II
E-Mail I & II
MP2000 Client Summary Inquiry
Attorney Profile & Expertise Bank
Case Management System
Client Guidelines
Expert Witness System
Practice Development System
Work Product / Brief Bank

Other EIA Series

Substantive Legal Programs (revive PCCLE)

Mastering the Personal Computer - Home & Office

Litigation Support

Overview of the Legal System for the PSS

Litigation Risk Analysis

Team Building

**Reinforce Standards Through a
MENTOR PROGRAM**

Reinforce EIA Standards

Provide Guidance in File Handling

Refine Client Development Practices

**Offer a "Safety Net" for Difficult
Situations**

EXCELLENCE IN ACTION - SECRETARY SERIES

Organizing Your Office
Professionalism & Business Ethics
Billing Guidelines & Procedures
Client Contact - Phones, Correspondence &
Face-to-Face
Opening & Closing Files
Managing Your Files
Preparation of Pleadings
Getting Assistance - Internal & External
Time Management
Stress Management

EXCELLENCE IN ACTION - PARALEGAL SERIES

Defining your Responsibilities
Professionalism & Business Ethics
Billing Guidelines & Procedures
Your Role with the Client
Managing Your Files
Preparation of Pleadings
Getting Assistance - Internal & External
Handling Complex Cases
Time Management
Stress Management

EXCELLENCE IN ACTION - ADMIN SERIES

Organizing Your Office
Professionalism & Business Ethics
Billing Guidelines & Procedures
Client Contact - Phones, Correspondence &
Face-to-Face
Opening & Closing Files
Managing Your Files
Preparation of Pleadings
Getting Assistance - Internal & External
Time Management
Stress Management

USING TECHNOLOGY - PSS SERIES

Phones, Phone Mail, Faxes & Equitrac
Word Processing I - IV
E-Mail I & II
MP2000 Time Entry & Client Summary Inquiry
Attorney Profile & Expertise Bank
Case Management System
Client Guidelines
Expert Witness System
Practice Development System
Work Product / Brief Bank

Graduation Luncheons in June

Awards and Recognition

Positive Impact on Performance Appraisal

Improved Profitability
Productivity Gains
Leverage Gains
Realization Gains

**Increased Client Satisfaction &
Retention**

Improved Competitive Position

Differentiation in the Marketplace

Improved Communication

Seize The Day!

CARPE DIEM

STANDARD MONTHLY AGENDA FOR SECTION MEETINGS

I   **Quality Discussion**
        A. Engagement Letters
        B. Action Plans
        C. End-of-Matter Report Cards
        D. Audits

II   **Education**
        A. Update Case Law, Statutes, Regulations, etc.
        B. Report on Seminars Attended, Given

III   **Case Information**
        For Litigation Sections
        A. Case Status
        B. Cases Tried During the Last Month
        C. Cases Settled During the Last Month
        For Nonlitigation Sections
        A. Discussion of Status of Open Matters
        B. Discussion of Matters Concluded

IV   **Business Development**
        A. Current Situation
           1. Review of Client Contact Sheets (Entertainment)
           2. Client Intelligence
           3. New Matters Received During the Past Month
        B. Long-Term Situation
           1. Existing Clients
           2. Cross-Marketing Opportunities
           3. New Clients —Targets

V   **Discuss Reports: (Production Billings Receivables)**

VI   **Analysis and Opinions (Specific Matters)**

VII   **Resolve Scheduling Conflicts**

VIII   **Administrative Items**

IX   **Special Projects**

X   **Old Business**

XI   **New Business**

XII   **For the Good of the Section**

Appendix
G

PLUNKETT & COONEY ATTORNEY PROFILE AND EXPERTISE SURVEY

Instructions: Please provide typed or neatly printed information only for those categories which are applicable. Please do not be an egoist on this. We want to know about things in which you have real expertise. Don't be shy either. Simply use good judgment and common sense.

NAME _____

I. **Principal areas of practice.** Here we want to know those areas of the law in which you believe you are most competent; e.g., insurance law, tax, environmental, etc.:

A _____

B _____

C _____

II. **Sub-Specialties.** Here we want to know those aspects of your principal practice in which you have significant experience, training, or knowledge; e.g., Insurance Law—Coverage Issues; Tax —Estate Planning; Environmental—Regulation; Professional Liability—Lawyers and Accountants:

A _____

B _____

C _____

III. **Substantive Law Specialties.** We want to know the points of *substantive* law on which you believe to possess special analytical expertise. The expertise may be limited to Michigan law only. If it is multi-jurisdictional, please indicate; e.g., Insurance Law—Coverage—Comprehensive General Liability policies; Professional Liability—Lawyers and Accountants; Statute of Limitations discovery rule Michigan and Ohio:

A _____

B _____

C _____

IV. **Procedural Law Specialties.** As with substantive law, we want to know those areas in which you have special legal expertise; e.g., jurisdiction—conflicts of law—Michigan, Texas; Appeals —interlocutory—Michigan, New York:

A _____

B _____

C _____

V.   **Evidence Specialties.** We want to know those areas of the law in which you have acquired special expertise; e.g., products liability—spoliation of evidence —presumptions:

A _____

B _____

C _____

VI.   **States of Licensure and Eligibility.** We want to know all states in which you are *licensed* to practice or in which you have knowledge of the law or experience that may make you a candidate for pro hoc vice admission.

A _____

B _____

C _____

VII.   **Name all Courts to which you are admitted to practice:**

A _____

B _____

C _____

VIII.   **Nonlegal Professional Degrees, Licenses, or Certifications.** We want to know all professions in which you possess recognized qualifications; e.g., Mechanical Engineering, B.S. (Univ. of Michigan 1975); Registered Nurse (Wayne State Univ. 1986); Civil Engineering, B.S. (Univ. of Detroit 1979); Registered Prof. Eng. - Michigan; Accounting, B.S. (Univ. of Detroit 1982); Certified Public Accountant - Michigan; Licensed Private Investigator - Illinois; Marketing, B.S. (Univ. of Nevada 1981):

A _____

B _____

C _____

IX.   **Amateur or Former Specialties.** We want to know about anything else in which you have acquired special know-ledge or training; or a former occupation in which you gained notable experience; e.g., former F.B.I. agent; former journeyman electrician; 10 years experience in numismatics; former Mayor, city of New York 1930-32; coach, minor league hockey 1976-80; team member Univ. of Michigan gymnastics team 1980, etc.:

A _____

B _____

C _____

X.   **Publications.** We want a list of all legal and/or non-legal articles, pamphlets, monographs, or books you have writ-ten or edited since entering college, and which have been published by a recognized publisher (including any uni-versity press) and/or any dissertation prepared to meet university degree requirements.

A _____

B _____

C _____

XI.   **Teaching.** We want to know about all of your teaching experiences, regardless of topic, inside and outside the law:

A _____

B _____

C _____

XII.   **Language Fluency.** Do not list any languages in which you are fluent if you have already done so in connection with the firm's recent survey. If you did not participate in that survey, list here *all* languages in which you are *fluent*. Indicate further whether you speak, write, or do business in the language:

A _____

B _____

C _____

XIII.   **History, Cultural, and Economic Expertise.** We want to know about any special knowledge of history, culture, and/or economics; e.g., France—history and culture only; Brazil—history, culture, and economics, etc:

A _____

B _____

C _____

XIV.   **Organizational and Management Experience.** We want to know what groups, companies, or other entities you have organized, managed, or led, of whatever nature or scope; e.g., department head, Ford Motor Company; Director, City of Detroit Waste Water Treatment Program 1987-88, etc.:

A _____

B _____

C _____

XV.   **Expert Lists.** We want to know those areas of professional expertise in which you have acquired familiarity with "experts" who are willing to consult for our clients; e.g., industrial safety; electrical engineering; banking; accounting; etc. Attach additional pages if need be:

A _____

B _____

C _____

XVI.   **Miscellaneous Expertise.** This is a catch-all category in which you can list any unique professional or nonprofessional activity in which you believe you have notable experience or knowledge; e.g., public speaking—Univ. of Detroit debate team 1969-71; commercial illustration; photography; etc:

A _____

B _____

C _____

XVII. **Recreational Activities.** We want to know what athletic or other recreational activities you regularly engage in and in which you have a high level of competence; e.g., golf (5 handicap), tennis, fishing, hunting, mountain climbing, karate, weight lifting. You name it, we want to know about it. *And let us know about any tournaments or trophies you have won.*

A _____

B_____

C _____

XVIII. **Educational Background.** Honors; awards; distinctions.

High School:_____

College: _____

Law School: _____

XIX. **Professional Organizations and Memberships.** Please list all professional organizations and memberships you hold or have held, including offices:

A _____

B_____

C _____

XX. **Civic, Charitable, or Special Interest Organizations.** Please list all organizations you have been involved with of whatever kind, nature, or description:

A _____

B_____

C _____

XXI. **Work History.** Please give a *complete* work history:

_____

_____

_____

_____

_____

_____

_____

_____

_____

ENDNOTES

Chapter 1

1. James A. Belasco, Ph.D., *Teaching the Elephant to Dance* (New York: Crown Publishing Group, 1990) 2.

Chapter 2

1. George Dixon and Julie Swiler, *Total Quality Handbook: The Executive Guide to the New American Way of Doing Business* (Minneapolis, Minn.: Lakewood Books, 1990).

2. Noel Tichy and Stratford Sherman, "Jack Welch's Lessons for success, GE: Control Your Destiny or Someone Else Will," *Fortune* 127 (25 Jan. 1993): 86.

3. James A. Belasco, Ph.D., *Teaching the Elephant to Dance* (New York: Crown Publishing Group, 1990) 166.

4. Situational Leadership II is a program developed by Blanchard Training and Development, Escondido, Calif.

Chapter 4

1. James A. Belasco, Ph.D., *Teaching the Elephant to Dance* (New York: Crown Publishing Group, 1990) 166.

2. 1992 Malcolm Baldrige National Quality Award Criteria.

3. Stephen Covey, *The Seven Habits of Highly Effective People* (New York: Simon & Schuster, 1989).

Chapter 5

1. Noel Tichy and Stratford Sherman, "Jack Welch's Lessons for success, GE: Control Your Destiny or Someone Else Will," *Fortune* 127 (25 Jan. 1993): 86.

2. Rosabeth Moss Kanter, "Managing the Human Side of Change," *The Organization Behavior Reader* (Englewood Cliffs, N.J.: Prentice-Hall, 1991) 675.

3. Kanter, "Managing the Human Side of Change," 675.

4. James A. Belasco, Ph.D., *Teaching the Elephant to Dance* (New York: Crown Publishing Group, 1990) 11.

5. James M. Kouzes and Barry Z. Posner, *The Leadership Challenge* (San Francisco: Jossey Bass, 1987) 79.

6. Belasco, *Teaching the Elephant to Dance*, 11.

7. Belasco, *Teaching the Elephant to Dance*, 127.

8. Belasco, *Teaching the Elephant to Dance*, 152.

9. Belasco, *Teaching the Elephant to Dance*, 166.

Chapter 7

1. On the perhaps erroneous assumption that you are not familiar with or are one of those who has forgotten the Rule:...when a person takes an estate of freehold, legally, or equitably, under a deed, will, or other writing, and in the same instrument, there is a limitation, by way of remainder, either with or without the interposition of another estate, of an interest of the same legal or equitable quality, to his heirs or heirs of his body, as a class of persons, to take in succession, from generation to generation, the limitation to the heirs entitles the ancestor to the whole estate. 4 Kent 215. This result would follow, although the deed might express that the first taker should have a life estate only. It is founded on the use of the technical words, "heirs" or "heirs of his body," in the deed or the will. *Hancock v. Butler*, 21 Tex. 804, 808 (1858).

2. Max DePree, *Leadership Is an Art* (New York: Dell Publishing, 1989).

3. Warren Bennis, *On Becoming a Leader* (Reading, Mass.: Addison-Wesley, 1989).

4. Cited in James A. Belasco, Ph.D., *Teaching the Elephant to Dance* (New York: Crown Publishing Group, 1990).

5. Stephen R. Covey, *Principle Centered Leadership* (New York: Summit Books, 1990).

6. Jan Carlzon, *Moments of Truth* (New York: Harper & Row, 1987).

7. Noel M. Tichey and Stratford Sherman, *Control Your Destiny or Someone Else Will* (New York: Doubleday, 1993).

8. Belasco, *Teaching the Elephant To Dance,* 2

9. Kenneth Blanchard, Ph.D., and Spenser Johnson, M.D., *One Minute Manager* (New York: Berkeley Books, 1982).

10. James M. Kouzes and Barry Z. Posner, *The Leadership Challenge* (San Francisco: Jossey-Bass, 1991).

11. Noel Tichy and Stratford Sherman, "Jack Welch's lessons for success, GE: Control Your Destiny or Someone Else Will," *Fortune* 127 (25 Jan. 1993): 86.

12. Belasco, *Teaching the Elephant to Dance,* 166.

13. Stephen Covey, *The Seven Habits of Highly Effective People* (New York: Simon & Schuster, 1989).

14. Belasco, *Teaching the Elephant to Dance,* 166.

15. Blanchard and Johnson, *One Minute Manager,* 1982.

16. Gordon F. Shea, *Mentoring* (Los Altos, Calif.: Crisp Publications, 1992).

Chapter 8

1. Kenneth Blanchard, Ph.D., and Spencer Johnson M.D., *One Minute Manager* (New York: Berkeley Books, 1982).

2. Paul Hersey, *The Situational Leader* (Eden Prairie, Minn.: Wilson Learning Corporation, 1984).

3. Kenneth Blanchard, *Leadership & the One-Minute Manager* (New York: William Morrow & Company, Inc., 1985).

Chapter 9

1. Roger K. Sullivan, BIS Strategic Decision, Presentation to the AIIM Executive Seminar on Electronic Image Management, 9 Oct. 1991.

2. Simon Chester, "Must Litigators Use Computers or Face Malpractice," *Winning with Computers: Trial Practice in the 21st Century* (Chicago: American Bar Association Section of Law Practice Management, 1991).

Joseph V. Walker is President and Chief Executive Officer of Plunkett & Cooney in Detroit, Michigan, the state's fifth largest law firm. He spearheads the development, continual training, and daily operation for the Excellence in Action program at the firm, working with firm lawyers, support staff, and clients. A graduate of the University of Detroit School of Law, Mr. Walker began his career as a law clerk at Plunkett & Cooney. He has promoted the use of total quality management principles and designed surveys tailored for in-house use at law and other service firms.

Barbara L. Ciaramitaro is Manager of Information Systems, Training & Development at Plunkett & Cooney. She is Phi Beta Kappa with a degree in psychology from Wayne State University. Her background includes over thirteen years experience in the many facets of technology and training in the legal environment. Her experience, insight, and commitment contributed significantly to the design and implementation of Plunkett & Cooney's Excellence in Action total quality program.

Action Steps to Marketing Success. Shows you how to turn your marketing ideas into action and run an ongoing, coordinated, results-oriented marketing program. Forms and sample letters included.

Anatomy of a Law Firm Merger. Provides information on every aspect of a merger and will help law firms of all sizes decide whether they should consider a merger.

Beyond the Billable Hour. A collection of articles on the subject of alternative billing methods, including value billing. Contributors include small, medium, and large firm practitioners, consultants, and general counsel.

Breaking Traditions. A guide to progressive, flexible, and sensible work alternatives for lawyers who want to balance the demand of the legal profession with other commitments. Model policy for childbirth and parenting leave is included.

From Yellow Pads to Computers, 2nd ed. Thirty-five chapters with real-life computer applications that focus on practical solutions. Especially for the attorney who's been too busy to use a computer.

How to Start and Build a Law Practice, 3rd Ed. Jay Foonberg's classic guide has been updated and expanded. Included are more than 10 new chapters on marketing, financing, automation, practicing from home, ethics and professional responsibility.

Improving Accounts Receivable Collection: A Practical System. Gives you the basics for developing an easy-to-manage, formal billing and collection system that can cut months off the collection process.

Keeping Happier Clients. Your guide to better client relations. It describes a whole approach to building strong relationships with clients. Includes questionnaires and tips for follow-up.

Last Frontier: Women Lawyers as Rainmakers. Explains why rainmaking is different for women than men and focuses on ways to improve these skills. Shares the experiences of four women who have successfully built their own practices.

Law Office Staff Manual, 2nd Ed. This updated version includes new sections on issues, techniques, and practices. Also includes the text of the manual on diskettes in WordPerfect and ASCII formats so that you can create a customized manual for your law firm.

LOCATE 1993-94. Listings of law office computer software vendors with indexes listing applications and package names.

Making Partner: A Guide for Law Firm Associates. Written by a managing partner, this book offers guidelines and recommendations designed to help you increase your chances of making partner.

Managing Partner 101: A Primer on Firm Leadership. Advice from the corner office that will help any new or aspiring manager. Described as an "indispensable handbook."

Marketing Your Practice. A complete guide for planning, developing, and implementing a law firm marketing plan. Includes checklists, questionnaires, samples of brochures, newsletters, and direct mail pieces.

Practical Systems: Tips for Organizing Your Law Office. It will help you get control of your in-box by outlining systems for managing daily work.

The Quality Pursuit. This multi-author work provides perspectives on a wide range of issues related to quality assurance and hgh performance standards, including dealing with the problem partner, partner peer review, training programs.

Results-Oriented Financial Management: A Guide to Successful Law Firm Financial Performance. How to manage "the numbers," from setting rates and computing billable hours to calculating net income and preparing the budget. Over 30 charts and statements to help you prepare reports.

A Short Course in Personal Computers. Explains the basic components of IBM-compatible computers in terms that are easy to understand. This concise and accessible guide will help you make knowledgeable decisions in the law office.

Winning with Computers, Part 1. Addresses virtually every aspect of the use of computers in litigation. You'll get an overview of products available and tips on how to put them to good use. For the beginning and advanced computer user.

Winning with Computers, Part 2. Expands on the ways you can use computers to manage the routine-and not so routine-aspects of your trial practice. Learn how to apply general purpose software and even how to have fun with your computer.

Win-Win Billing Strategies. Represents the first comprehensive analysis of what constitutes "value," and how to bill for it. You'll learn how to initiate and implement different billing methods that make sense for you and your client.

WordPerfect® in One Hour for Lawyers. This is a crash course in the most popular word processing software package used by lawyers. In four easy lessons, you'll learn the basic steps for getting a simple job done.

Your New Lawyer, 2nd Ed. A complete legal employer's guide to recruitment, development, and management of new lawyers. Updated to addresss the many changes in the practice of law since the 1983 edition.

THE SECTION OF LAW PRACTICE MANAGEMENT

Order Form

Qty	Title	LPM Price	Regular Price	Total
_____	Action Steps to Marketing Success (511-0300)	$ 29.95	$ 34.95	$_____
_____	Anatomy of a Law Firm Merger (511-0310)	44.95	54.95	$_____
_____	Beyond the Billable Hour (511-0260)	69.95	79.95	$_____
_____	Breaking Traditions (511-0320)	64.95	74.95	$_____
_____	From Yellow Pads to Computers, 2nd ed. (511-0289)	64.95	69.95	$_____
_____	How to Start & Build a Law Practice, 3rd ed. (511-0293)	32.95	39.95	$_____
_____	Improving Accounts Receivable Collection (511-0273)	39.95	49.95	$_____
_____	Keeping Happier Clients (511-0299)	19.95	29.95	$_____
_____	Last Frontier (511-0314)	9.95	14.95	$_____
_____	Law Office Staff Manual (511-0307)	79.00	89.00	$_____
_____	LOCATE 1993-94 (511-0321)	64.95	74.95	$_____
_____	Making Partner (511-0303)	14.95	19.95	$_____
_____	Managing Partner 101 (511-0272)	19.95	29.95	$_____
_____	Marketing Your Practice (511-0215)	44.95	54.95	$_____
_____	Practical Systems (511-0296)	24.95	34.95	$_____
_____	The Quality Pursuit (511-0268)	74.95	84.95	$_____
_____	Results-Oriented Financial Management (511-0319)	44.95	54.95	$_____
_____	A Short Course in Personal Computers (511-0302)	14.95	24.95	$_____
_____	Winning with Computers, Part 1 (511-0294)	89.95	99.95	$_____
_____	Winning with Computers, Part 2 (511-0315)	59.95	69.95	$_____
_____	Winning with Computers, Part 1 & 2 (511-0316)	124.90	144.90	$_____
_____	Win-Win Billing Strategies (511-0304)	89.95	99.95	$_____
_____	WordPerfect® in One Hour (511-0308)	9.95	14.95	$_____
_____	Your New Lawyer, 2nd ed. (511-0312)	74.95	84.95	$_____

*HANDLING

$ 2.00-$9.99	$2.00
10.00-24.99	$3.95
25.00-49.99	$4.95
50.00 +	$5.95

**TAX

DC residents add 6%
IL residents add 8.75%
IN residents add 5%
MD residents add 5%

SUBTOTAL: $_____
*HANDLING: $_____
**TAX: $_____

TOTAL: $_____

PAYMENT

____ Check enclosed (Payable to the ABA)   ____ Bill Me

____ Visa   ____ MasterCard   Account Number:_____-_____-_____-_____

Exp.Date: _____

Signature _____

Name_____

Firm_____

Address_____

City_____State_____ZIP_____

Phone number_____

Mail to: ABA, Order Fulfillment 511—9th Floor, 750 N. Lake Shore Drive, Chicago, Illinois 60611
Or FAX: (312) 988-5568

 **THE SECTION OF LAW PRACTICE MANAGEMENT**

CUSTOMER COMMENT FORM

Title of Book:_____

We've tried to make this publication as useful, accurate, and readable as possible. Please take 5 minutes to tell us if we succeeded. Your comments and suggestions will help us improve our publications. Thank you!

1. How did you acquire this publication:

☐ by mail order   ☐ at a meeting/convention   ☐ as a gift

☐ by phone order   ☐ at a bookstore   ☐ don't know

☐ other: (describe) _____

_____

Please rate this publication as follows:

	Excellent	Good	Fair	Poor	Not Applicable
Readability: Was the book easy to read and understand?	☐	☐	☐	☐	☐
Examples/Cases: Were they helpful, practical? Were there enough?	☐	☐	☐	☐	☐
Content: Did the book meet your expectations? Did it cover the subject adequately?	☐	☐	☐	☐	☐
Organization and clarity: Was the sequence of text logical? Was it easy to find what you wanted to know?	☐	☐	☐	☐	☐
Illustrations/forms/checklists: Were they clear and useful? Were there enough?	☐	☐	☐	☐	☐
Physical attractiveness: What did you think of the appearance of the publication (typesetting, printing, etc.)?	☐	☐	☐	☐	☐

Would you recommend this book to another attorney/administrator? ☐ Yes ☐ No

How could this publication be improved? What else would you like to see in it?

_____

_____

_____

Do you have other comments or suggestions? _____

_____

_____

Name _____

Firm/Company _____

Address _____

City/State/Zip _____

Phone _____

Firm Size: _____ Area of specialization: _____

We appreciate your time and help.

Fold

Fold